D1480610

ELECTRONIC RESOURCES:
ACCESS AND ISSUES

ELECTRONIC RESOURCES: ACCESS AND ISSUES

Mary Beth Fecko

Topics in Library and Information Studies

BOWKER
SAUR ●

London • Melbourne • Munich • New Providence, NJ

British Library Cataloguing in Publication Data
Fecko, Mary Beth
  Electronic resources : access and issues
  1. Online information services 2. Internet (Computer network)
  3. Document delivery – Data processing
  I. Title
  025'.04

  ISBN 1857390652

Z
692
.C65
F43
1997

Library of Congress Cataloging-in-Publication Data
Fecko, Mary Beth.
  Electronic resources : access and issues / Mary Beth Fecko.
    p.   cm. — (Topics in library and information studies)
  Includes bibliographical references (p.   ) and index.
  ISBN 1–85739–065–2   7
  1. Libraries—Special collections—Electronic information resources.
  I. Title.   II. Series.
  Z695.C65F43 1997
  025.17'4—dc21   97–24031
                                            CIP

Published by Bowker-Saur, Maypole House, Maypole Road, East Grinstead, West Sussex RH19 1HU, UK
Tel: +44(0)1342 330100 Fax: +44(0)1342 330191
E-mail: lis@bowker-saur.com
Internet Website: http://www.bowker-saur.com/service/

Bowker-Saur is part of REED BUSINESS INFORMATION.

ISBN 1–85739–065–2

Cover design by John Cole
Typesetting by Intype London Ltd
Printed on acid-free paper
Printed and bound in Great Britain by Antony Rowe Ltd., Wiltshire

TOPICS IN LIBRARY AND INFORMATION STUDIES

A series under the General Editorship of:

Charles L. Citroën,   Library, Delft University of Technology, Delft, The Netherlands
R.R. Powell,   Library and Information Science Program, Wayne State University, Detroit, Michigan, USA

Also available in this series:

Classification: Its Kinds, Elements, Systems, and Applications
D.W. Langridge

Acknowledgements

I dedicate this book to my husband, Rudy. I would like to acknowledge the contributions of my colleagues Norma Leo and Mila Su. They put in many hours reading my manuscript, offering suggestions, and verifying information. I would also like to thank my colleagues Ruth Dyer, Amelia Killough and Mary Edmonds for their emotional support while I was writing my manuscript.

Contents

Foreword by the General Editors

Without a doubt, one of today's most rapidly changing, pervasive, and publicized aspects of library and information studies must be electronic resources. In a relatively short period of time, electronic resources have expanded from a few dozen computerized bibliographic databases to include the overwhelming information available on the Internet. Use of electronic resources has moved from accessing online databases with a 'dumb terminal' to 'surfing' the World Wide Web with a high-speed, multimedia personal computer that has more power than early mainframe computers. The complexity of electronic resources has grown to include everything from electronic mail to virtual libraries. Electronic resources impact the producers, providers, and consumers of information.

With the explosion of electronic information resources, there is a pressing need for guidance in the use of such resources. Hence the inclusion of this volume in Topics in Library and Information Studies. Indeed, a book about electronic resources, written by a practising librarian with extensive experience in the area, is a natural for a monographic series aimed at an international audience of practitioners and students in library and information science.

Electronic Resources: Access and Issues brings to the consideration of electronic resources a treatment that is timely and topical. The preparation of the work commenced quite recently and the publisher expedited its production so as to provide a book as up-to-date as possible. The book, however, does cover some major aspects of the history of these applications. Other strengths of the book include its rather comprehensive scope. It addresses not only applications and background of the Internet, the Web, electronic publishing, and document delivery services, but also interactive multimedia and virtual libraries. Important to information professionals is the book's consideration of implications of electronic resources for library services, staff training, and collection development. The work includes extensive examples and references, both to print and online sources, and a glossary. In short, Mary Beth Fecko has written a book that should serve as a useful guide to the dynamic world of electronic resources. It is written in a language that makes it accessible to the novice, yet provides a level of detail that will meet many needs of the information professional struggling to cope with the complexities and issues of electronic resources.

Ronald R. Powell
Wayne State University

Charles L. Citroën
Delft University of Technology

Preface

This book is intended as a general introduction to how libraries use electronic resources. The electronic resources discussed in this text range from document delivery services to electronic mail to the Internet – including the multitude of resources available on the World Wide Web. Libraries are becoming increasingly automated and have begun to rely on electronic information to augment collections, or in some cases, to replace print resources. The purpose of this text is to explore some of the available electronic resources and to examine their impact on libraries, libraries' provision of information, and the way that library professionals and users respond to them.

In writing this book, I realized the difficulty of trying to describe the rapidly changing electronic environment in libraries. More quickly than in the past, new products, such as Microsoft Internet Explorer, and projects, such as the Elsevier Electronic Subscription service, are introduced as other resources become obsolete. Many long standing resources, particularly books and journals, are now available electronically. There is a chapter covering this topic, and it focuses on some of the current projects and publishers.

As I conducted research, I was surprised at the number of Web resources I used, ranging from Frequently Asked Question (FAQ) lists to full-blown research reports. Interestingly, some of the information I needed was available exclusively on the Web and had no print counterpart. Print indexes were incomplete or, in some cases, lacking information about Web resources and current projects but this information was available on the Web itself, which seems appropriate. Capturing details of Internet resources proved to be a challenge too, since several Uniform Resource Locators (URLs) have changed since I started to write, and at least two sites are now defunct.

Although I am a frequent library user, I must confess that I truly enjoyed using the Internet for some of my research. The two types of resources – print and the Web – produced different results for my research and different reactions from me. While I was overwhelmed by the volume of material I was able to obtain from the Internet, I often felt that I found more substantial information in printed journals, and I had to apply different search strategies to the two types of resources.

Chapter 1

Overview of the Evolution of Electronic Resources

Introduction

Computer-based automation was initially incorporated into library operations as a mechanism for handling the routine functions of running a library such as circulation, cataloging, acquisitions, interlibrary loan and serials control. Systems for handling these operations became available to the larger library community from the early 1970s onward, although there were some earlier pioneers with well developed local systems. Early systems were typically run on large computers into which data were entered, processed behind the scenes, and returned as printed output of some type (overdue notices, invoices, or catalog cards, for example). Pioneers in reference database services, such as DIALOG, also operated using large mainframe computers to which patrons connected via terminals and required experienced searchers mastering a complex set of commands to generate effective search results.

The introduction of the personal computer in the early 1980s heralded a set of major changes throughout the decade in the automation used by libraries. Databases were no longer necessarily housed at a remote site. Instead, they could be mounted on a machine at one's desk. Very little by today's standards could be done with those early personal computers. They lacked both storage capacity for holding and speed for processing large databases since they lacked hard disks, and used only floppies, had limited memory capacity, and used monochrome monitors. However, technology continued to improve rapidly. Improvements in speed and capacity made later developments, such as larger databases and enhanced search capabilities, possible. Several other technological developments during the 1980s had very significant effects on library automation: the introduction of computer files, particularly optical disc technology (CD-ROMS) as a data storage medium, the development and widespread deployment of networking hardware and software for linking multiple personal computers together (networks), and graphical user interfaces (GUIs). A GUI is an operating system which relies on icons, or pictures, rather than text only, to represent a file, directory, or functions (print, cut/paste, etc.) available on the system. GUIs require some type of windows interface (Microsoft Windows, RISC OS or NEXTSTEP, for example) to operate. Users typically access GUIs using a mouse or some type of pointing device. In contrast, a command line interface relies entirely on text. While Apple Computer claims responsibility for inventing the GUI for use with the Apple Macintosh operating system, it was Xerox's PARC laboratory that invented the concept during the 1970s (Howe, 1996).

Computer professionals continued to develop protocols that made it possible the growing number of networks throughout the world to communicate with each other and share information. This collection of interconnected networks and the actual resources available over these networks is commonly referred to as the Internet, or simply the Net. Text-based information retrieval tools (e.g., gopher, Veronica) to find information on the Net and file transfer protocol (FTP) to transfer files between networked computers were also introduced in the 1980s. These tools have been and continue to be routinely used by librarians to discover and retrieve Internet information. They will be discussed in Chapter Two.

During the 1990s technology has continued to develop, often faster than library professionals can realistically cope with it. Computers have increased power, speed, and capacity; monitors are larger and color is the norm; and networking capabilities have expanded. Increased power and improved graphics have led to more use of moving images and sound, requiring greater power and graphics to be effective. These features are now common on many of the popular databases, such as encyclopedias on CD-ROM. The ability to network effectively has led to the creation of more networks. More networks have led to a growth in electronic personal communications – e-mail – and a desire to share information and interact using the Net. Information is circulated much more quickly over the Internet and patrons are able to access the latest versions of information resources almost as soon as they become available. Currently there is a growth and a convergence of all of these technologies as applications begin to combine features to present a product to the user.

With so much information stored on networks and a desire to share that information, better access tools were developed which took advantage of the enhanced technology. In 1993, Mosaic, the first of a new generation of popular graphical information browsers was released with a version designed specifically for use with the personal computer. Mosaic captured the imagination of the larger computer world and a phenomenon was born. The early developers described the connected network of information resources as the World Wide Web (WWW) or simply the Web. Mosaic has since been succeeded by a new generation of Web browsers – Netscape Navigator, Microsoft Internet Explorer. Libraries with Internet connections provide access to these browsers which are used to search the Web for information on the Net. Search engines are used as a 'front end' or search mechanism for Web browsers. Many libraries make a variety of search engines available to their patrons. Different search engines offer different search techniques, displays of information, and other capabilities, and preference for a particular search engine varies with each patron's needs.

The array of electronic resources available in libraries today is an outgrowth of the changes in information delivery made possible through advances in both computer technologies, such as powerful personal desktop workstations, and information storage and delivery mechanisms, such as CD-ROMs and user-friendly GUIs. These advances make the ongoing efforts to replace other traditional services and processes with electronic versions attractive and economically feasible for many libraries. In most libraries, library information systems (LIS, for short, and formerly known as 'OPAC,' or online-public access catalog) have almost completely replaced card catalogs, offering enhanced search capabilities for accessing the local collection and often expand coverage to include the holdings of other area or regional libraries. Many libraries now provide a Web interface to their LIS, which means that access is provided through a graphical Web interface that works like an Internet search engine. An LIS with a Web interface often includes direct links to electronic journals, books and Internet resources. Libraries which do not provide Web interfaces to their LISs often find themselves in the position of having to both maintain a text interface and a Web page.

Indexes and abstracts on CD-ROM or available via a network have also become popular, transforming their print counterparts by making them easier and faster to use. The types of services and resources available in libraries have expanded far beyond basic reference service and traditional print based collections. Libraries have begun to offer services that include reference assistance via electronic mail, networked CD-ROM full-text databases, electronic reserve service, citation and document delivery services, Internet access, and Web pages with links to numerous online documents. Storing and transmitting information electronically has become the standard with these new services. Both information formats and delivery systems have changed rapidly in the past few years and many of the types of resources currently available far exceed what many librarians envisaged as possible only a few years ago. Technology, too, becomes outdated much more quickly due to the Internet's ability to make information available quickly to a large audience.

Public Services

Electronic resources are changing the longstanding relationship which traditionally existed between library professionals and users. Formerly, the use of resources and services required patrons to visit the library. Print indexes in the reference area provided needed citations, the card catalog indicated whether that library owned a particular item, and the circulation desk could place a hold for an item checked out to another patron. Early electronic tools such as DIALOG were available only to librarians who frequently consulted with users to refine their needs before conducting expensive and sometimes complex database searches. The introduction of large-scale automated union catalogs like OCLC have helped to revolutionize services such as interlibrary loan and library functions such as acquisitions and cataloging. The introduction of newer electronic resources have shifted services and functions from those which are librarian-mediated to those specifically geared towards the end-user. Advances such as the availability of online citation and document delivery services remotely accessed from a home or office, 24 hour remote availability to OPACs providing both an item's current circulation status and the ability to place holds oneself, plus the increasing number of resources available directly to patrons through networks, have combined to eliminate the need for a visit to the reference desk, or the library in many cases, to satisfy information needs.

Electronic resources permit patrons to be more self-reliant in their search for information. This shift in responsibility has led some large research libraries to institute reference service by appointment only. Basic questions, such as ready reference and directional questions, have been delegated to support staff at information desks. Despite these changes, the proliferation of electronic resources and the increase in end-user products will not bring about the demise of libraries or eliminate the need to visit libraries. Instead, the role of the library and the types of information and services it offers will be redefined. While the library's primary mission is still to provide information, the means for providing that information will change. As libraries continue to have the needs of patrons as their primary focus, they will also need to consider the quite different and conflicting needs of both on-site and remote patrons. The library's goal will be to provide information to patrons, yet the means to do so and personnel involved will shift as resources and needs change.

Planning for service

The emergence of electronic resources has led to an increased demand on libraries to deliver more in terms of services and products, and to do so faster. The enhanced services offered by libraries have raised the expectations of patrons. Technologically sophisticated patrons are frequently knowledgeable about new resources and their capabilities, often well before a library's staff. The versatility offered by electronic resources may also lead patrons to have unrealistic expectations about what technology can provide. They confuse the medium with the information.

The increasing availability of electronic information has required libraries to make difficult decisions regarding services and collections. Naturally, the most cost effective resources appropriate for the patrons of a particular library must be selected, but the choices now may include slightly different print and electronic versions of the same resource or different print and electronic resources that meet similar needs. Services must be redefined, and older, traditional resources and services may be eliminated so that newer electronic resources and services can be purchased and made available. This is not really a new phenomenon. Libraries have faced similar decisions in the past when new technologies such as microfilm were introduced. Librarians had to decide whether to select materials in these new media and how much to invest in the supporting technology, often at the expense of older resources and services. The most significant difference, however, is that none of the earlier new technologies made available as significant a share of mainstream information as have electronic resources. The fact that electronic resources are so pervasive means that for many libraries, these resources can neither be ignored (as microfilm sometimes was) nor relegated solely to niche services. Other factors, such as the rising cost of books and print journals, the decreasing availability of storage space in libraries for print materials, shrinking budgets, and theft and wear and tear of heavily used materials, make electronic resources an attractive alternative. Libraries are in the difficult position of attempting to accommodate the information needs of a wide variety of users, including the adventurous computer literate who resists print information, the technophobe who is unwilling to approach electronic resources, the traditionalist who takes comfort in printed formats, and the visual generation user who wants information to talk and move and be delivered in easily digestible sound bites. There may a temptation to ignore those users who do not readily embrace electronic resources and force them to fend for themselves. To do so would be a grave mistake and would send a very negative message on the part of the library. In a time when financial resources are dwindling, it is unwise to ignore any of a library's constituents (Vander Meer, Poole, and Van Valey, 1997, p. 28).

The increasing reliance on electronic resources is changing the nature of reference service and raises the following questions: What constitutes reference service? How will it be provided and to whom? Personalized reference service, in the traditional sense of individual contact with a live person, is becoming less common as automated processes and resources are better designed for end-users and contain fully realized assist features, navigational pointers, and links to other resources. This will allow end-users to access more information independently and to meet their information needs without librarian mediation. Many librarians are spending less time at the reference desk in order to provide services and assistance relating to electronic resources. Formerly, reference service typically included ready reference, instruction, and research-based reference. Lary (1995) suggests that reference service in the future will include instruction and guidance in '. . .1) accessing online information bases; 2) read-only data bases in read/write bases; 3) interactive video libraries; 4) interactive media production; 5) identification, comparison, evaluation, and supplying information in response to specific requests; and 6) conceptualizing and planning the production of curriculum-based products which automatically incorporate diverse learning styles.' Some of Lary's predictions have been instituted in libraries. For example, university libraries typically offer courses on how to search online databases; interactive computer terminals are becoming common at reference desks to provide maps, library tours, and answers to directional questions; LISs and Web pages are now frequently interactive; and the LIS or Web page provides access to databases.

The availability of electronic resources in libraries has changed the traditional longstanding links between professionals, information, and patrons. The introduction of products designed for end-users has decreased the need for librarians, or the library in some cases, to function as the intermediary in the information seeking process. A growing number of end-user citation and document delivery services, UnCover, for example, permit patrons to interact directly with them when requesting articles, completely bypassing the library in the process. While it may appear that electronic resources have freed up a great deal of the reference librarian's time, this is not true. Electronic resources have caused to librarians move away from direct provision of information to patrons to provide service in what initially appears to be an indirect manner. Time previously spent helping patrons may now be spent troubleshooting computer equipment, preparing guides and documentation for electronic resources, teaching the patrons how to use electronic information, establishing and monitoring in-house usage policies for electronic resources, developing and maintaining library Web pages, and answering reference questions via e-mail.

The introduction of electronic resources has led to a redefinition of reference service and how it will be provided. This is illustrated by the fact that many libraries have begun to offer reference service via electronic mail. Bristow notes that ' . . .this service will likely stimulate demand for other library services such as document delivery, databases beyond our own online catalogs, and expert systems designed within specific ranges of inquiry' (1992, p. 632). In an increasingly automated environment, there remain few individuals who do not use electronic resources for their work and communication. Even more conservative branches of librarianship, such as archives and special collections, have embraced the benefits provided by electronic resources for their daily work and professional networking. In many cases, there is no longer a choice as to whether one wants to use an electronic resource rather than a more traditional resource. Some library functions are almost exclusively carried out through the use of an electronic resource since institutions have done away with older technology in order to purchase newer technologies.

The nature of reference service has also changed in that ready reference, directional questions, and many of the simpler tasks have been delegated to support staff, and students in some cases. The fact that many questions can now be readily answered by documents available on local networks or mounted on Web pages has contributed to this downward movement of responsibilities. These electronic resources range from standard reference works such as dictionaries, encyclopedias, and almanacs to traditional vertical file material such as train schedules, maps, and job postings. Librarians are devoting a portion of their time to maintaining and updating their institution's electronic resources, developing local documentation mounted on in-house Web pages, designing user interfaces including LIS displays, and maintaining library Web pages which are likely to contain numerous links to other local and remote resources. Although online documentation may fulfill many of the information needs of patrons, a number of professionals are concerned that technology may reduce the opportunity for patrons to develop basic research skills which are often necessary when using traditional print resources. For example, patrons using full-text journal databases may never completely learn to use print indexes, how to locate print journals and back issues in a library, or how to use microforms or operate readers. They may end their search for information when an electronic resource fails to yield the desired information. These users may neglect the more traditional resources in libraries which offer a wide variety of information. Patrons may not sufficiently learn how to use a library's online catalog due to reliance on electronic and Web-based resources. They may not fully exploit a library's print resources because they are distracted by the lure of electronic resources which promise ease of use, GUIs, and quick return of information in many cases.

Professionals also have concerns regarding the loss of content of some print items when they become available in an electronic format. These resources omit important information, such as photographs or graphs when the electronic version is offered in a character-based format that lacks the graphical content of the original. Professionals are concerned that patrons may overlook the complete version (available in print) for the sake of convenience, forsaking content. An example of this is when the electronic resources offered by InfoTrac were first introduced in libraries. Patrons flocked to use InfoTrac, rather than standard print indexes, despite the fact that InfoTrac initially covered a very narrow range of years and the indexing was shallow. Patrons preferred what they found was a simple and convenient search session but which frequently yielded less information than a more involved search using a range of years in a standard print index.

An advantage of technology is that it can often pull together sources that formerly might only have been located using primary and secondary research sources. Some of the new databases and other technology include a variety of information for patrons, eliminating the need to do detailed research. Web browsers are easier to use than print indexes and other standard print search tools, for example. The increase in publications available on the Internet, including articles and conference papers, has made it convenient for patrons to obtain documents directly from online sources rather than locating articles through print indexes and making photocopies in a library. What patrons often fail to see is that a Web search may not be as specific as a search of standard print resources. And, while it may yield many hits, few of them may actually be relevant. In contrast, print indexes are very specific and contain a wider range of controlled subject headings. Patrons must define their searches, cross-reference topics, etc. to locate information. This part of the information seeking process (formulating a search strategy and using cross-references) is lost when using electronic resources. The controlled indexing vocabulary used for print indexes and subject headings has not always been used on the Internet. Information on the Web may not necessarily be the best or most current source of information. Patrons may, believe that what is available on the Web is the most current information and superior to print sources. This is not necessarily true since some Web sites are not regularly updated, and some sites are eventually abandoned altogether.

Notably, despite the availability of information on the Web and from networked databases, the majority of significant publications continue to be issued in print. Papers are being published and made available on the Internet and a number of electronic journal articles are available on the Web, yet there is a continuing trend to offer information in print. Many academics are reluctant to publish or make their work available on the Web since they feel it lacks prestige or proper authority. They are often unwilling to publish in a forum which provides little or no financial compensation, yet the same is also true for paper journals.

Training

The variety of electronic resources and types of new services currently available increases the importance of and need for education to enable end-users to take full advantage of the new opportunities available to them. Electronic resources are a significant investment in many libraries and it must be ensured that patrons are capable of getting a good return on that investment. Libraries must also confirm that they have spent their money wisely. It is not sufficient merely to make a resource available without also providing some form of training. While electronic resources may help to make patrons more self-reliant, they do not eliminate the need for training. There will continue to be questions that cannot be answered using electronic resources. Additionally, patrons will encounter problems and will require assistance while using electronic resources. The training that is offered must change to meet the new challenges and opportunities presented by electronic resources. Through user education, reference librarians are attempting to inform patrons of the existence of specific electronic resources, how to use them effectively, and to demonstrate their potential capabilities for solving information needs. In planning for training, the questions raised might include:

- How basic or detailed should training be?
- In what areas should training be provided?
- Should training include traditional print as well as electronic resources, particularly for those electronic resources with print counterparts in the library?
- Should basic training courses be mandatory for new students, or should it be provided only on request for specific courses?

Electronic resources require users to learn to search full-text multimedia and hypermedia systems, and also reinforces the need for training in more traditional skills, such as word processing, text editing, and using multiple search interfaces (Vander Meer, Poole, and Van Valey, 1997, p. 6). In answering these questions, libraries must examine their institutional commitment to and obligation for training, and plan accordingly.

Many libraries are also currently facing the challenge of how to reach the remote user who no longer or rarely enters the library. This differs from user education in that a direct plan or action or course is not provided. Remote users may access a library's LIS, citation or article databases, or a Web page. Providing assistance to these patrons requires well designed help screens and other documentation. Online documentation, including LIS displays, help files, finding aids, and Web pages, must be designed to effectively serve the needs of both on-site and remote users. The availability of specific resources can be promoted by creating catalog records containing clear pointers or links for connecting to the resources and including those records in the LIS.

Remote users fall into two classes: primary users who are affiliated with the library in some official way (a registered student using her university's library or a resident using his town's library) and secondary users who connect to the library from outside the primary community. Libraries have an obligation to meet the needs of their primary users. However, decisions must be made regarding how much and what type of help, if any, may be extended to secondary users. One option for libraries is to include online interactive tutorials on their Web pages. Some libraries offer help screens and virtual library tours on their Web pages

The availability of electronic resources through networks and the Internet has required libraries to examine their policies on information access. There are many more options that must be carefully weighed in an electronic environment. Electronic resources are often leased rather than purchased, and leased resources typically have contracts specifying which user community may access a resource and how many simultaneous users are permitted. Libraries must determine to whom access can be provided for which resources, how to comply with license restrictions, the appropriate level of commitment for a given resource, and where the library's responsibility ends, particularly for remote users. Some libraries are required to restrict the use of some resources to their own user communities and individuals who pay to use the resources on-site. Other resources can be freely used by anyone over a network. Mounting resources on Web pages is another option with its own set of issues concerning access and restrictions. Since libraries pride themselves on being providers of information, placing restrictions on access is often a difficult decision. In contrast, no library wants to be in the position in which demands placed on the system and resources by secondary users limit, or prevent, access for the library's primary clientele. A possible compromise may be for libraries to grant secondary users access for a fee or by special arrangement.

Collection development

The widespread availability of electronic resources, particularly those available on the Internet, will not diminish or eliminate the need for collection development. Collection development will begin to incorporate new challenges and concerns into the acquisition process, such as site licensing, copyright issues, and how access will be provided to various electronic resources. In a time of competing priorities and formats, and shrinking budgets, libraries must make difficult decisions regarding which resources are the most important and useful for their patrons, plus the necessary equipment to support them. LaGuardia and

Bentley (1992) recommend the following basic criteria for selection and purchase of resources:

- content;
- relevance;
- usefulness;
- cost;
- accessibility.

For research libraries, McBride (1993) reports that '...there is a growing realization that no research institution can sustain a self-sufficient collection into the indefinite future.... New electronic technologies allow revolutionary possibilities of uncoupling ownership from access, material object from its intellectual content.' This realization is applicable to most types of libraries. When planning for the acquisition and/or implementation of electronic resources, academic libraries must choose materials based on what is appropriate for the curriculum, the types of degrees conferred by the institution, and the type of research conducted by its faculty. Other factors to consider include:

- suitability of content;
- time span covered;
- frequency of update;
- to what extent a comparable print resource exists;
- compatibility with equipment owned by the library;
- searching capabilities of a particular resource

(Magrill and Corbin, 1989, p. 171).

Unlike print resources, decisions regarding the acquisition of electronic resources are directly tied to the availability of, or willingness to purchase, suitable technology to use the resource. Technology to support a resource cannot be separated from the resource itself. The selection process for an electronic resource may also take into consideration the amount of user instruction that will be required and the potential demands made upon the library's other services and resources.

When planning to purchase or make available an electronic resource, libraries should compare traditional and electronic forms of a resource in terms of cost, effectiveness, and anticipated usage. In terms of cost, the following questions might be raised:

- Which costs more?
- Can the initial purchase be overlooked in consideration of potential long-term benefits?
- Which resource will be more cost effective in the long run?

Ongoing costs such as subscriptions and maintenance must also be examined. In terms of usage, the following questions may be raised:

- Which is easier to use?
- Which will be preferred by the majority of patrons?
- What is the potential for use? Is there a demand for this type of resource?
- In terms of effectiveness, will an electronic resource 'perform' better than the print counterpart?

(LaGuardia, 1992, p. 61).

- Can the electronic resource manipulate data in a wider variety of desirable ways?
- What can it do that similar print resources cannot do?
- What can it not do that similar print resources can do?
- Does it have the potential to provide patrons with more timely information, and is it easy to use?
- Does it offer something different from anything which is currently available in a nonelectronic form?

After choosing which electronic resources to make available, a library must make commitments to those resources in terms of budget, maintenance, and promoting usage.

The availability of publications in electronic format has allowed libraries to re-examine and redesign other collection development practices. With the continuing growth of various full-text article databases, libraries may eventually consider acquiring materials on an as needed basis rather than proactively trying to anticipate user needs. Acquisitions would then be determined by immediate need. This suggestion is a radical departure from most standard collection development policies. Although many libraries have purchased a variety of electronic resources, most have not developed collection development policies that effectively address electronic resources. Instead, many libraries appear to have taken a 'wait and see' attitude towards electronic resources, preferring to wait and see which electronic resources are being used and how frequently, and what costs are involved. Rather than taking a proactive stance and preparing guidelines which may be modified accordingly as experience is gained using electronic resources, libraries attempt to build guidelines around the process.

Electronic resources offer great potential for resource sharing. CD-ROM products can be networked and shared on a local area network (LAN), for example. One CD-ROM can service a number of individuals at different locations, as compared to one print resource or a card catalog drawer, which can serve only one person at a time. Internet resources (Web sites, FTP and gopher sites) can store a great deal of information which may be accessed by hundreds of individuals worldwide. Indexing these resources through search engines and Web browsers increases their potential for use by informing patrons of their existence.

Digital collections of images also have great potential for resource sharing. They permit individuals to access resources or view exhibits and collections which they otherwise may not have the opportunity to see, due to distance or other factors. Projects such as the Global Campus, started by the California State University System, aims to share and make available through the Internet educational materials, such as images, sound, text, and video, (*About the global campus*, 1996) are examples of the potential for information sharing provided by the Internet. Digital collections offer a wider variety of uses for a resource than their print counterparts: a digital image of a manuscript, for example, may be marked up and altered by researchers a number of times, providing greater research possibilities.

Implications for library professionals

The proliferation of electronic resources has required library professionals to assume greater responsibility for keeping pace with technology. As the library becomes the provider of information in a variety of formats, it is essential that librarians know how to use the new technology required to access the information in those new formats, particularly when that technology has been made available to patrons whom the librarian may very well need to assist. A librarian who fails to keep pace with emerging technologies will be unable to adequately serve the basic information needs of library patrons. Keeping pace with changing technology has become a matter of necessity rather than choice. Before the widespread availability of resources on the Internet, it was often the case that the only individuals who were familiar with these resources were those with a keen interest in developing technologies, in contrast to those motivated out of necessity because of job requirements. The degree of knowledge and skill level required of librarians will be dictated by the needs and requirements of the institution, based on the kinds of information sources made available to support the curriculum the faculty research. Currently, librarians must often be familiar with both print and electronic versions of resources to help serve the information needs of several levels of patrons. It has already been suggested that the simpler reference tasks be delegated to support staff or student assistants when appropriate. This will allow the professionals to devote additional time to developing the necessary skills for effective service provision in this changing environment and to respond knowledgeably to the needs of the more sophisticated library patrons.

Some libraries have already started to move their professionals away from performing traditional services to concentrating almost exclusively on development and maintenance of the institution's electronic resources. This shift is not limited to public services librarians. In a presentation titled 'Technical Services Costs and Resource Allocation,' given at the American Library Association Annual Conference in New York, New York in 1996, Dilys Morris, Assistant Director for Technical Services, Iowa State University Library, explained that formerly forty percent of a professional's time was spent cataloging. A plan was devised to reallocate the division of labor in technical services, and professionals will now only catalog when their skills are needed. Professionals are devoting their time to developing electronic resources.

Clearly there will be a shift away from many traditional library practices which were once deemed as the core of library services and collections. Electronic resources have actually created more opportunities for patrons as well as the ability to customize services and resources to specifically meet their individual needs. For example, patrons can customize searches on the Web or in online databases, create bookmarks for frequently used Web resources, and make appointments for an in-depth research consultation with a librarian. The challenge for librarians will be to learn to strike a balance between collecting and providing access to print and electronic resources. In addition, librarians must keep in mind the needs of patrons as well as the resources of the library (both financial and personnel) as they build collections and prepare for access.

Chapter 2

The Internet and its Applications

Introduction

The Internet was barely acknowledged by the popular computing magazines in mid-1993 (Kriz, 1995). That situation changed within a year as the Internet began to make headlines in national news magazines, newspapers, comic strips, and television reports. Suddenly, everyone seemed to be talking about 'the Net,' Internet guides appeared in bookstores, Internet classes were offered by universities, colleges and libraries, and it was a popular topic for articles and conference presentations in a wide variety of disciplines. Even feature films and television programs included the Internet in themes and subplots. Internet applications, such as electronic mail, had been used since the 1980s, but interest in the Internet has grown phenomenally since 1994. This growth of interest can partly be attributed to the availability of affordable software for Windows (Kriz, 1996). The emergence of Internet providers such as America Online and CompuServe, combined with aggressive advertising campaigns, have helped bring the Internet into the mainstream. Internet providers created a market and convinced consumers that the Internet certainly had a place and purpose in their lives. The introduction of Web browsers, starting with Mosaic, also helped to make the Web more accessible, and easier to use and understand. It helped to bring order to the chaos.

To provide an idea of how activity on the Internet has grown, consider two quotes used by Gromov in his document *The roads and crossroads of Internet's history*. The first quote was taken from IBM: 'Nobody can say precisely how many people are using the Internet today, but there are estimated to be more than three million host computers with as many as 30 million users around the world. . . .' The second quote was taken from information contained in the *Domain-name database* (Imperative!, 1996): 'As of May 14th [1996], there are 325,444 total domains registered at the internic [sic] . . .190,225 domains have web sites (58% of the total).' In January 1997 there was a reported 57 million Internet users worldwide and 71 million people using e-mail (Language

Services International, 1997). As a point of information, the InterNIC is the Internet Network Information Center, which began in 1993 as a collaboration between AT&T, General Atomics, and Network Solutions, Inc. Today, InterNIC Registration Services is located at Network Solutions, Inc., in Herndon, VA and provides registration services for domain administrators, network coordinators, Internet service providers, and anyone else actively involved with the Internet. A domain refers to the suffix of a host computer's unique name that is assigned at the highest level and can be shared by other computers within an organization. For example, one computer's unique hostname might be "montanaro@rci.rutgers.edu" of which the suffix 'rutgers.edu' is the domain name shared by other computers within the same organization (e.g., fecko@rci.rutgers.edu, yseult@rci.rutgers.edu). Both the number of users and domains continue to grow steadily.

The Internet has provided access to a larger range of information than could ever be made available in one given library. It should be noted that while the terms 'Internet' and 'World Wide Web' (or 'the Web') are often used interchangeably, the two are not synonymous. The Internet is a network which connects many smaller networks worldwide; the Web is only a portion of the Internet. The Internet is most frequently used for reading and sending electronic mail, transferring files (file transfer protocol, or ftp), remote log-in, or telnet, and searching the Web. These functions will be discussed later in this chapter.

The growth of the Internet inspired many libraries to make documents and resources from their collections available online to the public as well as worldwide. LISs, local community information, bibliographic and citation databases, and electronic reference works were all made available through remote log-in. As more information became available, institutions increasingly competed to demonstrate who had made available the most comprehensive range of information. A library's status was no longer solely defined by the collection it housed; it was extended to include online resources which were easily available to remote users. Despite the wealth of information available on the Internet, there was little order to it. Individuals often found out about what a library had to offer through random searching and luck, word of mouth, or through professional literature. The plethora of information available on the Internet became more accessible via searching and indexing tools. Early tools, such as gopher, Jughead, and Veronica helped to give order to the chaos. File transfer protocol allowed users to import and transmit files. Telnet, or remote log-in, allowed individuals to tap into information available on remote computers. The World Wide Web and various Web browsers, such as Netscape Navigator and Microsoft Internet Explorer, along with new Web searching tools, comprised the next generation of Internet resources.

Electronic mail and other online services

Electronic mail

Electronic mail, or e-mail, allows people to send and receive messages using their computers. Each user has an e-mail address on a computer to which messages can be sent and a mailbox file (also on a computer) where the received messages can be stored until read by the recipient. E-mail has had a profound influence on the communication patterns of those who use it. It has helped to revolutionize the exchange of information. Prior to widespread use of the Internet, scholarly information was primarily disseminated through books and journal articles or shared at professional conferences. This sometimes meant that information was already dated by the time it was published and distributed to libraries. E-mail can be quickly and simultaneously distributed to a large audience. The ability to distribute time sensitive information to a large number of individuals in a timely manner is an added benefit for certain materials. For example, resources such as electronic journals permit timely scientific and medical information to be made available to the appropriate user communities much more quickly than using traditional channels (e.g., peer reviewed journals, proceedings, or books).

People communicate differently when using electronic mail. Standards have been relaxed somewhat, and individuals often feel free to voice their opinions in this faceless forum. Sherwood (1996) attributes the informal nature of electronic mail to the short turnaround time; she believes this makes electronic mail more conversational in style. In the absence of face-to-face communication, symbols and other stylistic methods are sometimes used to represent the missing facial expressions or tone of voice upon which we have come to rely for certain clues during interpersonal communication. For example, using all uppercase letters is believed to be the equivalent of shouting. Symbols include the use of emoticons (sometimes called 'smilies') such as :-) or :-(and stylistic forms include such things as tags ⟨HUMOR⟩ or ⟨SOAPBOX⟩...⟨END SOAPBOX⟩ to describe the nature of a message fragment.

E-mail has often been referred to as the 'great equalizer,' which in effect, means that all individuals are equal in this forum. For example, among e-mail participants in a professional discussion list, judgement about an individual develops over time based on the quality and content of that person's submissions and written contributions to discussion topics. Visual and aural cues, such as age, appearance or manner of speaking are not considerations in this forum, although writing style is clearly a significant factor. Interestingly, this contrasts with some recreational discussion lists and such interactive online games as Multi-User Domains (MUDs) or Multi-User Object Oriented Domains

(MOOs), where players often go to great lengths to describe their appearance (or more appropriately, fantasy appearance) for the game. A MUD is a multi-user game which is played over a network. A MOO is a text-based multi-user virtual reality game. In addition to entertainment value, MOOs have been used for educational purposes.

Discussion lists

In addition to sending and receiving individual messages, e-mail mailing lists are frequently used as the message distribution mechanism for electronic discussions lists or listservs. While 'listserv' is actually a user name taken from one of the early mailing list processors used to run many electronic discussion lists, it has become a commonly used shorthand term to refer to discussion lists themselves. A listserv is basically an automated mailing list dedicated to a particular issue or discipline. Generally, members subscribe to a list by submitting their e-mail address to the list software and via the software subsequently receive all messages posted to the list by other subscribers. Subscribers can also send messages to the other list subscribers, which is how they participate in the discussion. Alternately, some discussion lists are also available through Usenet which does not require individual e-mail subscriptions.

The number of postings to a list varies, depending on many factors, including the focus of the list, discussion topic, time of day, day of week, and even time of year. For example, traffic on many professional academic lists is normally slower in the summer and before major holidays; in contrast, a recreational vacation list may be quite active in the summer and before major holidays. Additionally, a focused professional discussion list may generate perhaps only a half dozen messages daily while an active recreational list might generate several hundred messages daily.

Discussion lists may be unmoderated or moderated. An unmoderated list redirects all incoming mail messages to the list of recipients. They are not monitored and often have an 'anything goes' flavor. A moderated list is actively monitored by a list owner or designated moderator who sets policies, and edits and filters messages. Messages posted to a moderated list are filtered by humans before being redirected to subscribers. A list's tone is often set by the moderator. News posted to listservs travels quickly and reaches a wide audience (worldwide, in many cases). Job postings, industry news, conference announcements, and obituaries are examples of the types of news posted to listservs. Typical postings include questions and requests for information on how to solve a particular problem.

In the early 1990s, there was an incredible variety of lists which met a multitude of professional and personal needs, ranging from library professional lists (including separate lists for acquisitions, reference, collection development, circulation, interlibrary loan, and cataloging) to other professional lists (autism, sports psychology), literature lists (children's literature, mysteries), food lists (gourmet food, low-fat foods), recreation lists (films, travel) and sports (bicycling, scuba diving). Some lists were short lived and eventually became inactive or obsolete as interest in a particular topic died, or as list owners realized they lacked the time, computer space, or institutional support to operate an active listserv. In addition, subscribers often became bored with a topic or overwhelmed by the volume of mail received from listservs.

Several sites maintain records of current discussion lists which are available in several different ways. A few which are cited in the American Association of School Librarians (1996) will be described. To receive an e-mail message containing a list of listservs, send an e-mail request to 'listserv@searn.sunet.se' without a subject line, containing only the message 'list global,' followed by part of a subject term relevant to your interest (e.g., list global chem). As of October, 1996, this list had approximately 9000 entries taking more than 27 000 lines. By June 1997, this list had grown to 13 050 entries. The large size makes it impossible for the site to return the full list without expending more resources than the list owners are willing to commit to an individual request; hence, the need to limit searches to a general subject area. This same list of listservs may also be searched on the Web through the 'CataList' interface provided by L-Soft International at http://www.lsoft.com/lists/listref.html. A comprehensive list of scholarly and professional discussion lists maintained by Kovacs et al. (1996) can be accessed either through the gopher at the University of Saskatchewan at gopher://gopher.usask.ca or through the Web at http://n2h2.com/KOVACS/. Rob Kabacoff (1996) at Nova Southeastern University also maintains Web links to several lists of electronic mailing list discussion groups (including Kovacs et al. (1996) mentioned above) at http://www.nova.edu/Inter-Links/. Another source is the list of publicly available mailing lists compiled by Stephanie da Silva (1996) and available through NeoSoft at http://www.neosoft.com/internet/paml/index.html.

Librarians have taken advantage of the communication and networking benefits offered by listservs and electronic mail. Discussion lists have made it possible for professionals to communicate broadly and quickly with others, and to share ideas and plan in a group setting in ways that were not possible using older technologies. An example of how communication and scholarly networking have been changed through e-mail and later the Web may be demonstrated by the case of the electronic journal *LIBRES: Library and Information Science Research Electronic Journal*. The editorial board was organized through a call for volunteers posted to several professional listservs. Most of the editorial board was selected from among the respondents to that call, and an online editors' planning conference was conducted electronically following selection of the editorial board. The journal conducts all business (calls for submission, peer review of submissions, and communications to the board) using the Internet. Editorial board members are located worldwide, ranging from the United States to Australia. Without electronic mail, organization of an editorial board for a peer-reviewed scholarly journal would have taken much, longer particularly for one with international participation. Previously, calls for volunteers might have been posted in professional journals, solicited at professional conferences, or editors might have relied upon recommendations from colleagues. In contrast, *LIBRES: Library and Information Science Research Electronic Journal* was operational in a fairly short timeframe. This type of progress would not have been possible without electronic mail. Electronic mail has fostered communication and relationships between professionals who otherwise would not have met and who may possibly never meet face-to-face. Name recognition and professional reputation have easily become part of the communications revolution. In many cases, professionals are already well acquainted with each other through the Internet, and yet have never met in person. Electronic mail has led to a new way for professionals to network and exchange information and ideas.

Bulletin boards
Bulletin board systems (BBS) are another Internet application based on shared electronic messages. A bulletin board consists of a computer and related software that provide an electronic database where users can log-in and leave messages or read messages left by others (Howe, 1996). Messages are frequently grouped by topic as a BBS gets large enough (i.e., when there is a sufficient volume of messages on diverse topics) and anyone can submit or read a message. Bulletin boards were first used in the early 1980s, and were used as message bases (Naples Area Bulletin Board System Operators, 1996). Users carried on conversations by posting messages to each other, and participation was international. Traditionally, most BBSs are small operations run by amateur hobbyists out of their homes although a number of larger commercial and educational systems exist today; other than the commercial systems, most are free. Bulletin boards are still used mainly for conversation and, in that respect, are similar to electronic mail 'chat rooms.' Other services may be provided, including file archives, application programs, games, and graphic image files. Public domain and shareware programs and software often appear on bulletin boards for distribution shortly after release by their authors (Howe, 1996; Naples Area Bulletin Board System Operators, 1996).

Usenet

Usenet, also referred to as Netnews, is a collection of hundreds of bulletin boards which use a common distribution method and similar software to post and read messages. The individual bulletin boards are generally known as newsgroups, or simply 'groups.' They are distributed through a loose network of host computers, called newsfeeds, which carry some subset of the available newsgroups. Only the largest of the newsfeeds might decide to devote enough resources to carry all available groups; most feeds only carry some subset of the available groups although that subset could be quite extensive.

To participate in a specific newsgroup individuals must connect to a newsfeed that carries that particular group. Each newsgroup is devoted to discussion of a given topic which could be quite narrow in scope or very broad, and new groups are constantly being created. In general, most newsgroup names try to reflect the discussion topic to make it easier for readers to identify that group. Newsgroup names contain a hierarchy of elements separated by periods. The first element is based on the general category under which the group should be classified. For example, newsgroups beginning with the word 'alt' are for alternative groups (alt.activism, alt.alien.visitors, alt.archery); newsgroups beginning with 'biz' are about business and commercial activities (biz.book.technical, biz.jobs.offered). Further divisions in the name are designed to focus in on the specific topic of the group while at the same time organizing the group alphabetically with others sharing similar topics. For example, 'rec.collecting' groups are all under the recreation hierarchy and discuss different areas of collecting (rec.collecting.coins, rec.collecting.dolls, rec.collecting.sport.baseball, rec.collecting.stamps). A newsgroup can have many elements to its name hierarchy (for example, comp.infosystems.www.authoring.html), and will contain as many as necessary to distinguish the group from other similar groups while organizing it alphabetically close to those groups.

Usenet allows users that have installed news feeder software on their computers to read and post messages or to read articles from the newsfeed to which they have connected. Messages may be cross-posted to several newsgroups. Newsgroups may also be moderated or unmoderated, which can affect the number and quality of the postings to the group. The newsfeed can be accessed through telnet or the World Wide Web. Many of the most popular Web browsers include news reading software. A sample of some of the available newsgroups can be found on the World Wide Web at World Wide Web Consortium (1995) at http://www.w3.org/pub/WWW/Newsgroups.html.

Freenets

Freenets are community-based information systems that offer services ranging from e-mail to information services, interactive communications, and conferencing (Howe, 1996). This resource started as a way to introduce the public to local Internet-accessible resources, and are funded and operated by volunteers. Freenets offer access to local libraries, local government resources, and other community-oriented services. They are a low or no-cost alternative to Internet providers. It is often difficult to access a freenet since the volume of users can be high. For this reason some freenets have started to restrict their services to certain classes of users, usually those within their local area. Access to freenets is often through telnet, but it is also available in some cases through the Internet (gopher and the World Wide Web). Text-based freenets available via telnet have been superseded by easy to use and visually oriented Web sites. Probably the best known freenet is the Cleveland Freenet. An extensive list of freenets and other community networks is available from Scott (1996) at http://duke.usask.ca/~scottp/free.html. Examples of a Web-based freenet are shown in figures 2.1-2.5.

Internet indexing and retrieval tools

Gopher

The increasing availability of information on the Internet and the corresponding lack of indexing and access tools led to the creation of searching tools like gopher. Gopher was one of the earliest attempts to provide organized access to information available on the Internet, and is an example of a distributed document retrieval system. With a system like this, distribution of information belonging to a collection of different databases or information systems is transparent to users, and appears to function as one local system. Distributed systems typically rely on client-server applications. In a client-server system, software has both 'client' and 'server' functions. The client is a computer that requests a service from another computer; the server is a computer which provides a service to the computer making the request. Gopher started as the University of Minnesota's campuswide information system, and consists of menu-driven software that 'tunnels' through the Internet for information. Information in gopher is organized in a hierarchy of subject-oriented menus. The menus provide links to text files, other menus, binary files, FTP sites, telnet sites, and Z39.50 sites (Internet Public Library, 1996). Gopher sites concentrate on different areas of information to meet the various information needs of users. There are sites on such diverse topics as aging, Russian history, health sciences, and international monuments and sites.

In the early 1990s, gopher was heralded as the newest electronic resource. The excitement created by this new resource started a rush to establish gopher sites to make available an institution's resources.

Figure 2.1 Freenet (Web-based) Electronic Village of Abingdon.
Source: *http://www.eva.org*

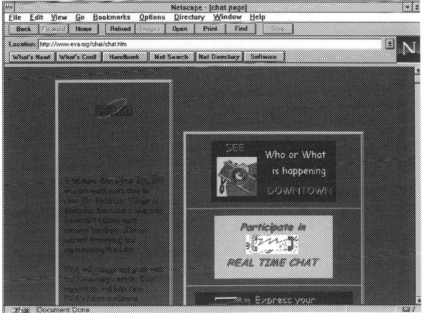

Figure 2.2 Freenet (Web-based) Electronic Village of Abingdon.
Source: http://www.eva.org

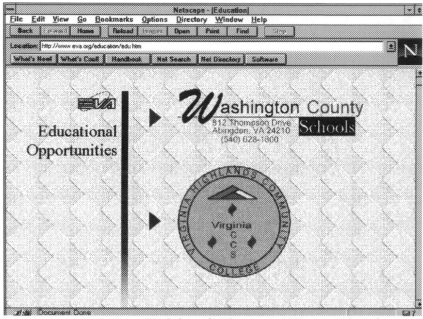

Figure 2.3   Freenet (Web-based) Electronic Village of Abingdon
Source: *http://www.eva.org*

Figure 2.4   Freenet (Web-based) Electronic Village of Abingdon
Source: *http://www.eva.org*

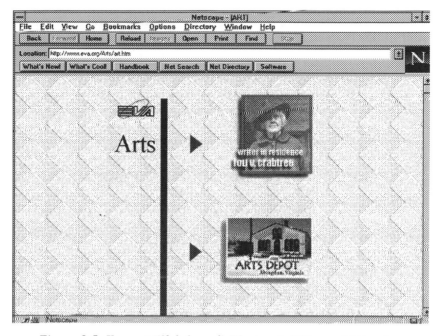

Figure 2.5 Freenet (Web-based) Electronic Village of Abingdon
Source: *http://www.eva.org*

Listservs were filled with messages about various gopher sites and how to access them. The growing number of gopher sites was accompanied by an increased need to provide indexing to the information available at the sites. This led to the development of Veronica, an indexing tool for gopher menus which is often found on the 'other gophers' menu. The name Veronica stands for 'Very Easy Rodent-Oriented Net-wide Index to Computerized Archives.' Veronica maintains an index of gopher menu titles and uses keywords to search those titles, and establishes electronic connections to provide access. In this sense, Veronica was like a precursor to hypertext links.

Gopher was also assisted by Jughead, a database of gopher links. Jughead stands for 'Jonzy's Universal Gopher Hierarch Excavation and Display,' and was developed in 1993 by the University of Utah Computer Center. It indexes all gopher sites, but provides access only to high-level menu items. Access is not provided for menus of file names.

Eventually, gopher gave way to the World Wide Web. GUIs and ease of use made the Web more attractive to users than gopher's text-based menu displays (which often required a good deal of navigation). It should be noted, however, that gopher is one of the access schemes currently available on the Web. The World Wide Web will be discussed later in this chapter.

File transfer protocol

File Transfer Protocol, more commonly known as FTP, is another Internet application. It is a client-server protocol that allows users to transfer files to and from one computer to another via a Transmission Control Protocol/Internet Protocol (TCP/IP) network. TCP/IP is the group of protocols used to connect computers and to send data over a network. FTP uses the TCP/IP protocols to transfer files. It allows users to transfer files between any two computers of any type (PC to PC, PC to mainframe, PC to Mac, or PC to Unix machine, for example) (Kriz, 1996).

The first large-scale library experiment in cataloging online resources, conducted by OCLC in 1992, was largely accomplished by transferring files via FTP. Participants first obtained instructions and information files to catalog from an OCLC computer using FTP. They later submitted test catalog records and accompanying log files to OCLC via FTP. This experiment was the first of its kind and was quite revolutionary. It established a model for later cataloging experiments and future projects in general. It also demonstrated the viability of using FTP to transfer catalog records in routine processing, a record exchange option that has been subsequently been made available by the large bibliographic utilities (OCLC, RLIN).

Users may also access files using Anonymous FTP, an interactive service available through Internet hosts (hosts are the domain name following the 'at' (@) sign portion of an Internet address) that allows users to transfer documents, files, programs, and other archived data using FTP. Users log onto a site as 'ftp' or 'anonymous,' and use 'guest,' or more often their personal e-mail address, as the password. Access is granted to a 'special directory hierarchy containing the publicly accessible files, typically in a subdirectory called "pub"' (Howe, 1996). This subdirectory is usually separate from files accessed by public users.

Implementation of FTP led to the development of archie, which provides an indexed dictionary of all anonymous FTP archives on the Internet. Archie was initially implemented by the McGill University School of Computer Science. It can be accessed interactively through telnet or by using client software on a mainframe. Archie allows users to search multiple Internet archives using one interface. This service may be used to locate data, text, or program files. The database contains names of all archie files, plus a description is given for each file. The archie database is available on a number of archie servers which contain the same information. A list of archie services is maintained by Nexor (1997) at http://pubweb.nexor.co.uk/archie/. Archie may also be accessed by e-mail at archie@archie.mcgill.ca using the single word message 'help'. Archie may be accessed via e-mail in the United Kingdom at archie@uk.ac.ic.doc (Bostock, 1997).

Telnet and Hytelnet

Telnet is another Internet service and is a protocol that allows users to log onto a remote computer. The remote computer is referred to as the 'host.' Using telnet allows an individual's computer to become a terminal connected to the remote computer through a process called 'terminal emulation.' Terminal emulators are programs which allow a computer to work like, or emulate, a specific type of terminal that is recognized by the host. 'The computer thus appears as a terminal to the host computer and accepts the same escape sequences for functions' (Howe, 1996).

Telnet is most commonly used to search LISs and databases mounted on local networks. The advantage of using telnet is that users can directly search another library's LIS and bypass asking a librarian for assistance. LISs are often a more accurate and detailed reflection of a library's collection when compared to how its holdings might appear in national bibliographic utilities like RLIN and OCLC. This information provides remote users with a more complete understanding of the other library's collection.

Hytelnet developed by Peter Scott of the University of Saskatchewan Libraries, is ' . . .a hypertext browser that allows a user to gain almost instant access to all telnet-accessible sites on the Internet' (Scott, 1992, p. 15). Browsers are programs which allow users to read hypertext and to navigate between sites. Hytelnet includes access to library catalogs, archie, databases and bibliographies, freenets, fee-based services, and NASA databases. This browser was initially written for IBM compatible PCs, and can be used from an individual workstation. Versions have since been written for Macintosh, Windows, Unix, and VMS systems. Since Hytelnet uses hypertext, there is no need for hierarchical menus used by schemes such as gopher. The database can be downloaded and locally stored, and users may add new information to the local version. A Unix version of Hytelnet is available for trial use at access.uskask.ca (log in as 'hytelnet'). The database may also be located on http://www.cc.ukans.edu/hytelnet_html/START.TXT.html.

WAIS

Wide Area Information Server (WAIS), is another distributed information retrieval system. It was originally released in 1991 and was designed specifically for maintaining and searching databases. This system can retrieve information from the Internet using natural language searching and allows users to search a number of sites simultaneously. It uses the Z39.50 information retrieval protocol (National Information Standards Organization (US), 1995) and can exchange information with other databases that have implemented the Z39.50 protocol. Z39.50 is at present the best technology for providing a single user interface for multiple information resources that are available via the Internet. 'Its purpose is to allow one computer operating in a client mode to perform information retrieval queries against another computer acting as an information server' (Lynch, 1991).

WAIS searches produce a list of documents ranked according to the frequency of occurrence of the keyword(s) used in the search. This ranked retrieval is combined with a relevance feedback capability to help refine future searches (Howe, 1996). Searching is simplified in part by allowing searchers to query several sites simultaneously without using different search terms or language specific to each site; this is one of the advantages of this distributed information retrieval system. Many WAIS servers are available on the Internet. Users who have only electronic mail access use WAISmail@quake.think.com to gain access to the database.

World Wide Web

The World Wide Web, or the Web for short (also referred to as WWW or W3 in certain contexts), was first proposed in 1989 by Tim Berners-Lee of the European Particle Physics Laboratory known as CERN. It was originally planned as a networked hypertext system to transmit documents and to communicate between members of the high-energy physics community. The Web has evolved to include sound and video capabilities, and the ability to transmit images. The flavor of the Web has changed from that of a vehicle primarily used for the exchange of scholarly information to a multi-faceted resource used for entertainment, travel, and general purpose information. Additionally, the Web has become increasingly commercialized and includes ads for Internet providers, search engines and software, long-distance telephone service providers, and even automobiles.

The Web is an example of a client-server application. Web browsers, or 'clients,' request information from Web servers. The server sends the appropriate information to the computer which has made the request. The type of information most frequently found on the Web includes:

- scientific and technical information (current research, abstracts of papers, for example);
- popular culture and entertainment;
- opinions; and
- PR-type company information

(Ryan, 1996, p. 17).

Historical information, information on the humanities, and proprietary company information are much less likely to be found on the Web (Ryan, 1996, p. 18). This is a reflection of the types of individuals who continue to contribute to, and use, the Web. Ease of use has made the Web very popular, as compared to other Internet resources, such as gopher. The Web is analogous to television in that it relies on the power of visuals. Individuals have become visually oriented by years of exposure to television. Like television, the Web has provided users access to places and resources which they otherwise might not get a chance to visit or see.

The Web uses hypertext to provide access to documents and navigation between documents. Hypertext consists of links that allow users to move from one document to another through use of programs called browsers. Browsers enable users to view the contents of hypertext links. Interestingly, some professionals have likened hypertext links between Web documents to footnotes and bibliographic references. The advantage of these hypertext links over traditional footnotes and references is that they provide direct and immediate access to related documents.

No real rules or standards exist for Web documents although standardized practices or conventions often emerge over time within a particular user community. Individuals create and maintain their own documents, and a variety of styles, formats, and information are exhibited by the myriad Web documents. Hughes (1994) comprehensively outlines what is available on the Web:

- anything served through gopher, WAIS, or anonymous FTP;
- full archie (FTP), Veronica (gopher), CSO, X.500 and 'whois' services, and 'full finger' services (whois and finger services are Internet directory services used to look up individuals' names on remote servers (Howe, 1996));
- anything on Usenet, in Hytelnet, techinfo, textinfo (campuswide information systems) or hyper-g (an Internet information system for multimedia data), or anything accessible through telnet;
- HTML-formatted hypertext and hypermedia documents.

Web browsers

Access to the Web is provided by browsers, which are programs that allow users to search for information, and to view pages, documents, etc. on the Web. Browsers are available on individual workstations, and allow users to send a request to a server or to follow links provided in a document or site. The most popular browsers today are all graphical although there are some character-based browsers available for users without the level of equipment to support a resource-intensive graphical browser. Lynx, Mosaic, Netscape Navigator, and Microsoft Internet Explorer are all browsers. Many of the most common browsers make their software available free individuals or at minimal cost. Users who have access to the Internet but lack access to browsers can access the Web through telnet by using the command telnet www.w3.org (Howe,

1996). Many Web sites offer text-based access for those users with older computers with slower communications capabilities and which lack access to necessary browers.

Lynx is the most common browser used for text-based Web access (i.e., without a graphical interface). It was developed at the University of Kansas, and is designed ' . . .for use on cursor-addressable, character cell terminals or terminals under UNIX or VMS' (Howe, 1996). A user generally encounters such terminals when using a VT 100 terminal or a software package on a PC or MAC that runs a VT 100 emulator (e.g., Kermit, ProComm, etc.). More information about obtaining the most current version of the Lynx client and access to Lynx user guides can be found at Grewal (1996) at http://222.crl.com/ subir/lynx.html.

Netscape Navigator and Microsoft Internet Explorer, among others, provide graphical capability for browsing. 'Graphical World Wide Web clients enable publication of data over the Internet in a manner which allows the user to view text, color graphics, sound, and video in a manner that approaches the usability, and surpassed the functionality of a printed magazine' (Kriz, 1996). Mosaic was the first multimedia graphical user interface to the Internet and was developed by Marc Andreesen and Eric Bina at the National Center for Supercomputing Applications (NCSA). An early version of Mosaic was first made available in 1993. Part of Mosaic's success was due to early availability to test versions.

Some of the features which Mosaic introduced (which are now common to graphical Web browsers) included a mouse-driven GUI, the ability to display hypertext and hypermedia documents, ability to display electronic text in a variety of fonts, support for sound, ability to display characters as defined in the ISO 8859 character set (including languages such as French, German, and Spanish), support for movies (MPEG-1 and QuickTime), provided interactive forms support, support for interactive graphics up to 256 colors, and the ability to make basic hypermedia links to and support FTP, gopher, telnet, NNTP, and WAIS (Hughes, 1994).

With graphical Web browsers, users may selectively 'bookmark' resources which they are viewing. Bookmarking adds the electronic address and generally an associated name of the displayed resource to a local file to which the user can subsequently refer. This file then contains direct links to selected electronic addresses of previously viewed documents. Connecting to a resource from the bookmarks file allows a user to quickly and easily access a previously viewed document to which he wishes to return. However, there is a tendency for users to create many bookmarks for sites which they may rarely (if ever) use again. A general rule of thumb is that bookmarks should be reserved for frequently consulted sites.

Mosaic was the first graphical successor to earlier text-based software such as FTP and gopher. However, in the rapidly changing early browser marketplace, Mosaic was quickly overtaken by Netscape Navigator, another graphical Web browser, when its additional bells and whistles captured the attention of many users. It is produced by Netscape Communications Corporation, and Marc Andreesen, who originally helped develop Mosaic, is one of the authors of Netscape. Some of the features currently offered by Netscape Navigator include:

- ability to bookmark, including the ability to hierarchically arrange bookmarks through the use of headers;
- support for sound formats;
- ability to access video formats;
- a Virtual Reality Modeling Language (VRML) viewer that allows users to run three-dimensional applications;
- integrated e-mail access;
- direct access to newsgroups;
- CoolTalk, an Internet telephone tool;
- supports FTP uploads and downloads;
- supports a variety of graphics, including JPEG (a format for compressing color or gray-scale digital images) and GIF (a standard for compressing digitized images);
- support for Java applets (programs written in the Java programming language which can be distributed as an attachment to a Web document) and programs on a number of platforms, including Macintosh, Windows 95 and NT, Sun Solaris and SunOS, and IBM AIX.

More information about the availability of the various Netscape Navigator clients can be found at Netscape Communications Corporation (1997) at http://home.netscape.com/comprod/products/navigator/index.html.

One of the newest Web browsers to capture a significant market share is Microsoft Internet Explorer, which was initially released in late 1995, and is a current rival to the dominance of Netscape Navigator. Microsoft Internet Explorer has a variety of features, including:

- the ability to customize searching (size and position of toolbar can be changed, favorite sites can be organized into folders);
- a rating system for sites;
- multilanguage support (currently the only browser to do that, according to Microsoft's Web page);
- communications functions (electronic mail and access to Netnews);
- multimedia capabilities.

At this time, Microsoft Internet Explorer is currently available for Microsoft Windows (including Windows 95 and Windows NT) and Apple Macintosh platforms. More information on Microsoft Internet

Explorer may be located at Microsoft Corporation (1996) at http://
www.microsoft.com/ie/.

Markup languages

Standard Generalized markup language

Standard Generalized Markup Language (SGML) is a standard for
electronic information exchange. It was first produced in 1988, and was
initially used by organizations with special or complex requirements
for document management, such as the United States Department of
Defense, the Association of American Publishers, Hewlett-Packard, and
Kodak (Marchal, 1996). SGML can be used in two ways:

* for publishing, from single medium conventional publishing to
  online multimedia database publishing; and
* to produce files which may be read by others and exchanged
  between machines and applications

(SGML Project, 1996).

This standard may be used by individuals to write their own markup
schemes. SGML uses descriptive markup that indicates the nature, function, or content of the data; it does not indicate how data should be
processed. Marchal (1996) stresses that SGML is not limited to textual
applications, and has also been used for structured electronic data
exchange. The most popular application of SGML is Hypertext Markup
Language (HTML).

HTML and Uniform Resource Locators (URLs)

Hypertext Markup Language (HTML) is a document format. Invented by Tim Berners-Lee, HTML is '...a collection of platform-
independent styles (indicated by markup tags) that define the various
components of a World Wide Web document' (National Center for
Supercomputing Applications, 1996). HTML documents are plain text
or ASCII files and can be created using any text editor, such as emacs
(Unix), BBEdit (Macintosh), or Notepad (Windows). Tags are used to
indicate the different parts or elements of an HTML document.
Elements are part of the structure of a text document, and may contain
plain text, other elements, or both. Elements are used for headings,
tables, paragraphs, or lists. Tags contain a left angle bracket, a tag name,
and a right angle bracket. An example of a tag used for a title would
look like this: ⟨HEADER⟩. Tags are usually paired, and include start and
end instructions. The end tag differs from the start tag in that a slash
precedes the text in brackets, for example, ⟨TITLE⟩Document⟨/TITLE⟩.
HTML is not case sensitive, and tag information does not necessarily
have to be in all uppercase or lowercase. Web browsers do not support

all tags and will ignore those which they do not support (National Center for Supercomputing Applications, 1996). The required tags for most documents will include heading, title, and body of document. No recorded or 'official' rules exist for the creation or presentation of Web documents. Individuals create and update their own documents, which exhibit a variety of styles, formats, and information. HTML allows document creators to manipulate visual elements (fonts, font size, or paragraph spacing, for example) without changing the original information. 'The current HTML standard supports basic hypermedia document creation and layout, but is limited in its capability to support many complex layout techniques found in traditional document publishing' (Hughes, 1996).

The Web relies on Uniform Resource Locators (URLs) to specify the location of an object on the Internet. URLs are often thought of as 'Web addresses.' It is an item's URL that is saved as its 'electronic address' in the bookmark file discussed earlier in this chapter. Each URL address is divided into segments with the first segment (the portion of the address before the first colon) specifying the specific access scheme or protocol under which the rest of the address is structured. For example, some of the Internet protocols that have been cited previously in this text include 'telnet,' 'gopher,' and FTP. Information following the colon is interpreted according to access scheme. Addresses for many, but not all, of the most common access schemes used on the Web consist of two slashes following the colon followed by a hostname and a path to a specific resource. http://wfn-shop.Princeton.EDU/foldoc/ provides an example. This structure can be seen in nearly all of the online sources listed in the bibliography at the end of this book. Most of those references follow the HyperText Transfer Protocol scheme, or 'http,' as seen in the above example. Other example of schemes include 'WAIS,' 'news,' 'telnet,' or 'mailto' (Howe, 1996). Punctuation, spacing (or lack of spacing), and capitalization are extremely important in an URL address and should be transcribed exactly as found. Some computers will interpret addresses with different capitalization as different resources. Notice that the above example address includes a dash, several periods, several forward slashes, and both upper- and lowercase letters.

Virtual Reality Modeling Language

Another standard currently used for Web documents is Virtual Reality Modeling Language (VRML). It was written by Mark Pesce in 1993, and is a standard for authoring, viewing, and hyperlinking three-dimensional images on the Web. Despite its name VRML is not virtual reality, nor is it an extension of HTML, but a way to access three-dimensional objects over the Web.

VRML files are called 'worlds,' and have .wrl as their extension.

'These worlds contain exhaustive scened descriptions complete with detailed specifications of all the elements in the world' (Meroz, 1995). The most popular VRML browsers are WebSpace and WorldView. Current use of VRML is primarily for entertainment, education, art, and sciences. Meroz (1995) believes that future applications will provide a much more transparent user interface, and more interactive, collaborative applications such as virtual conferencing. For more information on VRML, consult the VRML Repository (1997) at http://www.sdsc.edu/vrml/ or Toni Emerson's *VRML Bibliography* (Emerson, 1997) at http://www.hitl.washington.edu/projects/knowledge_base/vrml_bibliography.html.

Guidelines for Creation and Maintenance of Web documents

McClements and Becker in their article 'Writing Web page standards' (1996) have produced concise standards and guidelines for creation and maintenance of Web documents. The guidelines derive specifically from their experiences at the University of Wisconsin-Madison library system and synthesize many elements found elsewhere in the literature as well. Their standards consist of three parts: content, design, and procedural/technical concerns. The following information is based upon the suggestions given in this article followed by responses from the author.

Content of Web pages

McClements and Becker (1996) make the following suggestions for keeping Web pages current:

1. Use a copyright statement or indicate the latest date of update. *Response*: This is important, particularly for individuals citing the Web page as a source of information. It also lets users know the currency of information that they are using. Similar information is provided for books and journal articles. This type of information is just as essential for Web documents which change frequently or are updated on an ongoing basis. (see Figure 2.6.).

2. Provide a statement of status when a document is in progress (an 'Under construction,' sign, for example). *Response*: This lets users know what will be available, and possibly when. Since Web documents changes frequently, this type of information is necessary. It provides users with a preview of what may follow, similar to prepublication publicity.

3. Include a section highlighting new information, content, etc. *Response*: This alerts users when new information is added to the Web

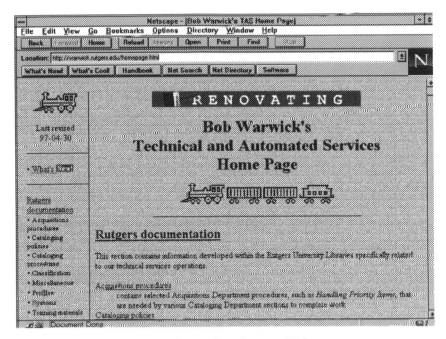

Figure 2.6 Date of update on Web page.
Source: *http://warwick.rutgers.edu*

page, and also benefits infrequent users. This type of information is important for digital collections that feature exhibits, which may change, move, or conclude. Inclusion of this information follows the same type of principle as that which is used when new editions of books are advertised. (see Figure 2.7).

4. Provide an indication of restricted access when appropriate.
Response: This is consistent with other library policies that restrict access to services, collections or locations. The indication should consider the needs of all categories of users (primary, secondary, and remote) when their restrictions vary by category (see Figure 2.8).

5. Include a warning statement when links will lead to large documents or images. *Response*: Warning statements are particularly important when users have limited computing power or time, and allows them initially to make better informed decisions about accessing the resource. This is particularly helpful when an estimated time to load is included.

Design of Web pages
The following should be considered for the design of Web pages:

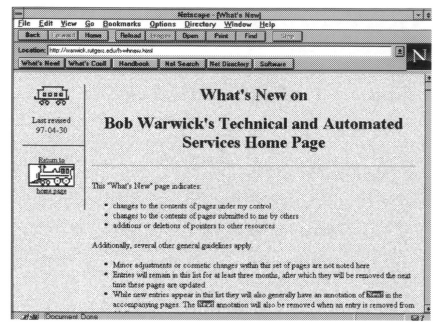

Figure 2.7 Indication of new contents.
Source: *http://warwick.rutgers.edu*

1. Use a style sheet for visual consistency across related documents.
Response: Consistency makes for ease of use within the related documents of a resource and aids user navigation. A jumble of documents that appear to be unrelated or which radically differ in appearance and content will hinder, rather than help, users. A good source for beginning to explore style sheets available from the World Wide Web Consortium (1996) at http://www.w3.org/pub/WWW/Style/.

2. Use small graphics to identify all of the documents on a Web site.
Response: Including small graphics is similar to providing a table of contents, and permits users to see what is available rather than their having to navigate several pages of content. They can be used to provide structure and reinforce the visual elements of the Web without detracting from textual content.

3. Offer a short and simple home page. *Response*: Simplicity makes for ease of use. A home page is the introductory document of a Web site or document, and includes the site's main Uniform Resource Locator (URL). Home pages often include statements of purpose, dates, contact

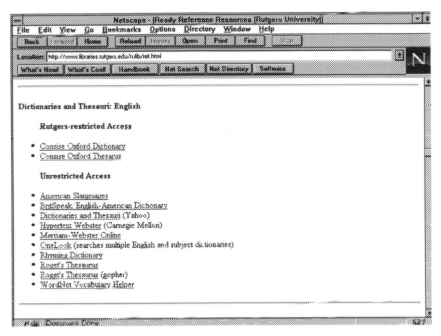

Netscape - [Ready Reference Resources [Rutgers University]]

File Edit View Go Bookmarks Options Directory Window Help

Back | | Home | Reload | | Open | Print | Find | | |

Location: http://www.libraries.rutgers.edu/rulib/ref.html

What's New! | What's Cool | Handbook | Net Search | Net Directory | Software

Dictionaries and Thesauri: English

Rutgers-restricted Access

* Consise Oxford Dictionary
* Consise Oxford Thesarus

Unrestricted Access

* American Slanguages
* BritSpeak: English-American Dictionary
* Dictionaries and Thesauri (Yahoo)
* Hypertext Webster (Carnegie Mellon)
* Merriam-Webster Online
* OneLook (searches multiple English and subject dictionaries)
* Rhyming Dictionary
* Roget's Thesaurus
* Roget's Thesaurus (gopher)
* WordNet Vocabulary Helper

Figure 2.8 Restrictions on access warning on Web page.
Source: *http://www.librarieseva.rutgers.edu*

information, or introductory pages to the Web site. Additionally the home page will be used as a future point of reference for users, and should include links to various documents at the Web site.

4. Provide active links to mentioned documents. *Response*: This is very important for resources that take full advantage of the Web as an interconnected collection of information pieces. Links should be maintained, and reviewed often for currency and accuracy. Otherwise, with broken links, many Web documents can quickly become useless. Unusable links are also bad PR for the institution or agency that has produced the Web document, and call into question the credibility of the site.

5. Avoid 'monster' graphics, as well as using many little graphics; sparingly use bold, italics, blinking, etc. *Response*: While it is true that the Web is a highly visual medium, one should avoid overpowering a page with very large graphics or cluttering it with many different small graphics. With experience, this recommendation can be balanced with the above recommendation of using small graphics for document identification. Emphasis should be on content of information, not presentation. The presentation from the page should not detract from content or impede access.

6. Provide navigational aids for users; provide hot buttons for short cuts. *Response*: Provide as much information as possible in the form of regular and consistent visual and written clues to help users navigate within a resource and to move around within the collection of informational pages forming that resource. Clickable links to previous and next sections, back to the table of contents, or home page, are helpful. Avoid users getting 'lost' in documents. Documents should be arranged in a logical fashion and be relatively easy to use.

7. Use a minimum of text in lists or menus. *Response*: Simplicity makes for ease of use. Sustained reading from computer screens is difficult, and users may turn away. An abundance of text may be overwhelming, and the Web document may not seem user-friendly. Reduce clutter to maximize use.

Procedural and technical specifications for Web documents
The following recommendations concern procedural and technical specifications for Web documents:

1. Use a markup language that is readable by future maintainers of the Web site or page. *Response*: Most organizational resources made available on the Web are intended to outlast the responsibility of the original designer. This recommendation helps assure a smooth transition when the eventual change in responsibility occurs. It keeps options open and flexible (see Figure 2.9).

2. Check the finished document with a variety of browsers, both textual and graphic. *Response*: Testing is important and essential. It is necessary to ensure that everything is functioning properly. Additionally, testing should be conducted on an ongoing basis.

3. Restrict development to nonpublic directories. *Response*: Keep development areas private. Do not provide access to the public. Beta test sites may be provided for users, but development in general should be restricted to private use.

Lastly, McClements and Becker (1996) stress for all three areas of consideration the importance of testing with a primary user group. While a specific resource may well appeal to a wide range of users, it is critical that the resource be most useful to its primary users. Web resource development in organizations has a function and a purpose most closely related to its intended primary users group and its success

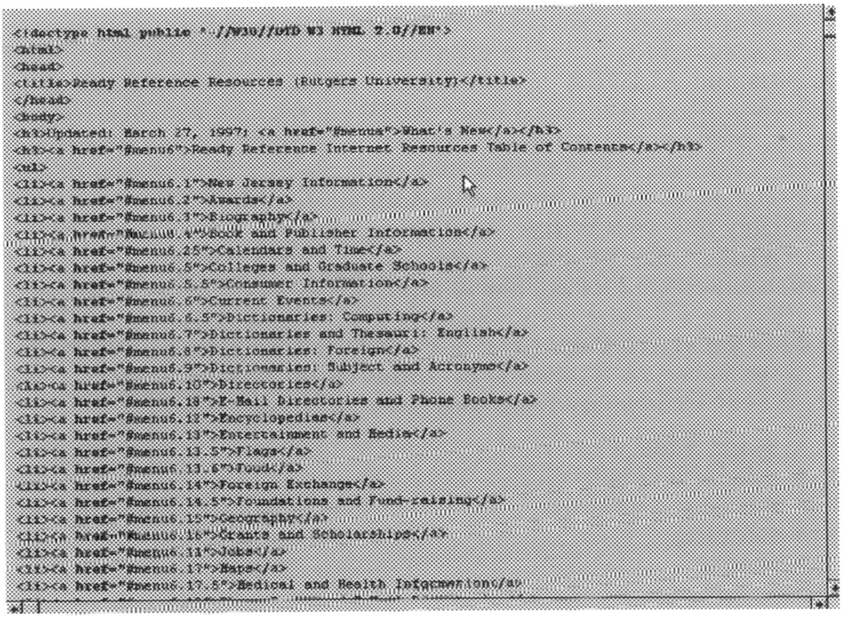

```
<!doctype html public "-//W3O//DTD W3 HTML 2.0//EN">
<html>
<head>
<title>Ready Reference Resources (Rutgers University)</title>
</head>
<body>
<h3>Updated: March 27, 1997; <a href="#menu4">What's New</a></h3>
<h3><a href="#menu6">Ready Reference Internet Resources Table of Contents</a></h3>
<ul>
<li><a href="#menu6.1">New Jersey Information</a>
<li><a href="#menu6.2">Awards</a>
<li><a href="#menu6.3">Biography</a>
<li><a href="#menu6.4">Book and Publisher Information</a>
<li><a href="#menu6.25">Calendars and Time</a>
<li><a href="#menu6.5">Colleges and Graduate Schools</a>
<li><a href="#menu6.5.5">Consumer Information</a>
<li><a href="#menu6.6">Current Events</a>
<li><a href="#menu6.6.5">Dictionaries: Computing</a>
<li><a href="#menu6.7">Dictionaries and Thesauri: English</a>
<li><a href="#menu6.8">Dictionaries: Foreign</a>
<li><a href="#menu6.9">Dictionaries: Subject and Acronyms</a>
<li><a href="#menu6.10">Directories</a>
<li><a href="#menu6.18">E-Mail Directories and Phone Books</a>
<li><a href="#menu6.12">Encyclopedias</a>
<li><a href="#menu6.13">Entertainment and Media</a>
<li><a href="#menu6.13.5">Flags</a>
<li><a href="#menu6.13.6">Food</a>
<li><a href="#menu6.14">Foreign Exchange</a>
<li><a href="#menu6.14.5">Foundations and Fund-raising</a>
<li><a href="#menu6.15">Geography</a>
<li><a href="#menu6.16">Grants and Scholarships</a>
<li><a href="#menu6.11">Jobs</a>
<li><a href="#menu6.17">Maps</a>
<li><a href="#menu6.17.5">Medical and Health Information</a>
```

Figure 2.9 HTML coded document.

or failure is largely measured by how successfully it has met the needs of those primary users.

Search engines, Internet catalogs, and other Internet resources

'A search engine proper is a database and the tools to generate that database and search it; a catalog is an organizational method and related database plus the tools generating it' (Grossman, 1996). Lycos and Alta Vista are examples of search engines. In contrast, Yahoo is a directory of information which uses Alta Vista's search engine to provide access to its contents.

The following descriptions of some useful Internet resources demonstrate the variety of both search engines and directories that can help library professionals and users access the variety of information currently available on the Internet. These resources continue to develop as the Internet grows and changes, and are representative of the most popular tools available today.

ALIWEB ALIWEB is a search engine that was created in 1993 to fill the services provided by Web harvesters and wanderers without putting a strain on network and processing resources. Harvesters and wanders, also known as spiders, are programs that retrieve documents from a

Web site, plus all documents referenced in that particular site. Individuals register their sites for inclusion in the ALIWEB database. After registration, ALIWEB retrieves their files and includes them in its database, which is updated daily. ALIWEB may be searched by substring, whole word, or regular expression. Searchers may indicate if a term is case sensitive. Searches may be limited by organization or site, information, document, or service. Additionally, ALIWEB provides the capability to search by title, description, URL, or other fields. Consult ALIWEB's welcome page (1995) at http://www.nexor. co.uk/public/aliweb/aliweb.html for additional information. (see Figures 2.10–2.11).

All-In-One Search Page   Created by William Cross (1996), All-In-One is a grouping of a variety of forms-based Internet search tools. Resources are organized into the following broad categories:

- World Wide Web;
- general Internet;
- specialized Internet;
- software;
- people;
- news/weather;
- publications/literature;
- technical reports;
- documentation;
- desk reference;
- other interesting searches/services.

The categories are further subdivided into search engines and various resources. The specialized Internet category, for example, provides access to resources such as AstroNet, Compaq Web servers, the Discovery Channel Online, and the IBM Web server. The listing is quite comprehensive, and entries for resources experiencing problems are annotated with a reason and date rather than removed (e.g., '9/12/96: Service is temporarily unavailable' or ' 8/17/96 : No response from server, possibly down.') Additional information on All-In-One may be located at Cross (1996) at http://www.albany.net/allinone. (see Figure 2.12.).

Alta Vista   This search engine was created by Digital Equipment Corporation, and according to Digital, provides access to the largest Web index by tapping into 30 million pages found on 275600 servers, and four million articles from 14000 Usenet news groups (Digital Equipment Corporation, 1996). Alta Vista is accessible through any standard Web browser, solicits site submissions, and is updated once daily. After users specify a search, Alta Vista produces a prioritized list of all the Web pages that contain search terms from the query. The system uses a

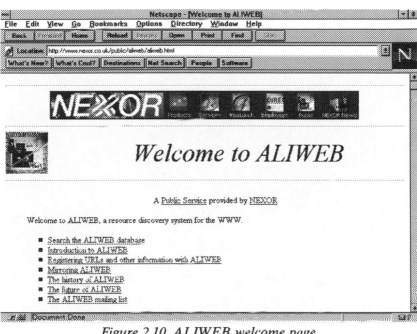

Figure 2.10 ALIWEB welcome page.
Source: webmaster@nexor.co.uk

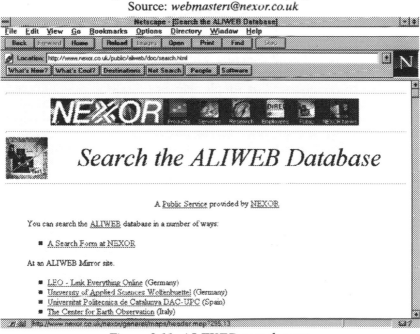

Figure 2.11 ALIWEB search page.
Source: webmaster@nexor.co.uk

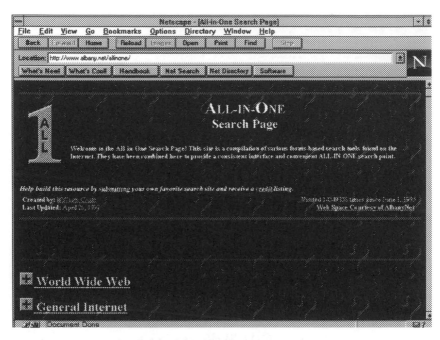

Figure 2.12   All-In-One Search Page.
Source: *wcross@albany.net*

ranking system to prioritize matching resources based on how many of the user's search terms it contains, where those terms are in the document, and their proximity to each other. Alta Vista provides the capability to do advanced or simple searches. Boolean operators may be used with the advanced searching features, and start and end dates for desired information may be included. Alta Vista has several mirror sites in Europe and provides access through a variety of European languages, plus a mirror site in Australia and a beta mirror site in Malaysia. More information on Alta Vista may be located from the main Alta Vista search page (Digital Equipment Corporation, 1996) at http://www.altavista.digital.com. (see Figure 2.13).

Argus Clearinghouse This subject guide to the Internet was formerly known as the *Clearinghouse for subject-oriented internet resource guides.* It was originally started at the University of Michigan in 1993 as an academic venture. The Clearinghouse holds or points to over 400 guides to Internet-based information resources. Guides are created and maintained by individual contributors who are subject experts on various topics. Broad subject categories include the arts and entertainment, business and employment, education, humanities, and science. All

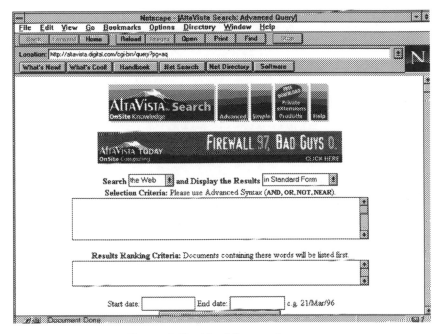

Figure 2.13 Alta Vista main page.
Source: *altavista-web@altavista.digital.com.*
Reproduced with the permission of Digital Equipment Corporation. Alta Vista
and the Alta Vista logo and the Digital logo are trademarks of Digital Equipment
Corporation

guides are available free, and are rated on such criteria as level of resource description, level of resource evaluation, guide design, and guide organizational schemes. One goal of the Clearinghouse is to rate all guides that it accepts but the task is not yet complete. Information on the Argus Clearinghouse may be located from Argus Associates, Inc. at http://www.clearinghouse.net/ (see Figure 2.14).

Cyberhound Cyberhound is a search engine which relies on manual indexing of Internet sites by editors. Sites are reviewed by editors using standard rating criteria developed by CyberHound that consider content, design, technical merit, and entertainment value. Users can choose to search all sites, Web pages, gopher sites, FTP sites, or telnet sites. Search criteria may focus on full-text, site name, URL, description, time span, site organizers, or subject terms. Searches may be customized to search by resource:

- databases;
- discussion groups;

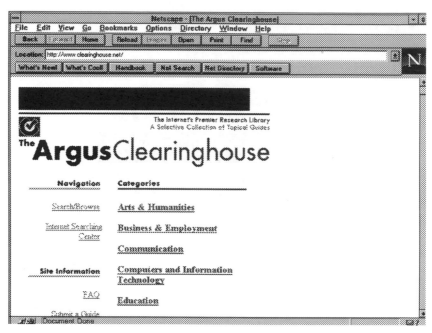

Figure 2.14 The Argus Clearinghouse main page.
Source: *info@argus-inc.com*

- libraries;
- publications;
- personal sites;
- associations;
- the who's who database;
- pop culture Web pages.

Searches may be limited to all areas, or broad subject areas such as arts, business, education, etc. Information on CyberHound may be located through the Gale's CyberHound home page at http://www.thomson.com/ cyberhound.default. (see Figures 2.15.)

Deja News Although Deja News is not a search engine or catalogue but a World Wide Web interface to Usenet newsgroups which allows users to search Usenet postings as well as read and post to Usenet newsgroups. Users can search newsgroup postings, and use 'author profiling' to see to which newsgroups a particular person (i.e., a particular e-mail address) has posted. Deja News provides a Usenet browser for users to search newsgroups. Deja News archives Usenet postings, and users can search them by keyword, filter for certain criteria

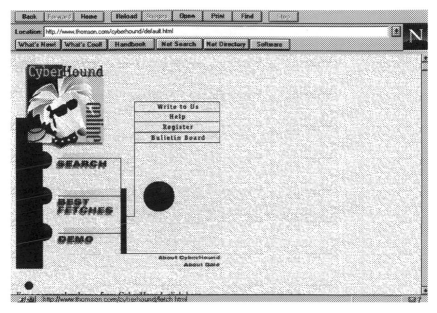

Figure 2.15 CyberHound main page.
Source: *woof@gale.com*

(newsgroup, data, author, subject), or use query profiling to locate newsgroups where specified keywords appear most often. Information on Deja News may be located at Deja News, Inc. (1997) at http://www.dejanews.com/. (see Figure 2.16.)

Excite Excite is an Internet navigation service which searches and summarizes more than 50 million Web pages and more than two weeks of Usenet news, includes over 61000 reviews written by professional journalists, and provides an hourly news update by Reuters. Excite includes site reviews, City.Net (information on top cities, maps, and travel planning information), ExciteSeeing Tours (a synopsis of information on the Web), Excite Reference (Yellow Pages, People Finder, Email lookup, maps). Excite Live! allows users to create their own personal Web guides according to their specific interests. Browsing features such as Query-By-Example and Sort-By-Site and advanced searching techniques are available. Information on Excite may be located from its home page at http://www.excite.com/. (see Figures 2.17–2.18).

Galaxy Galaxy is a directory and search engine. As with the Argus Clearinghouse, the Galaxy Directory is divided into broad categories

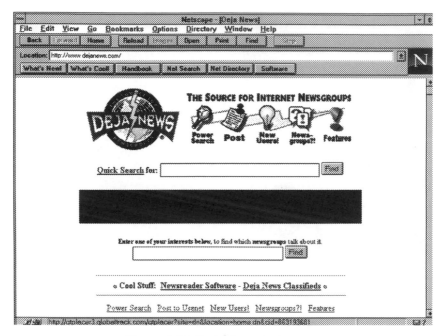

Figure 2.16 DejaNews main page.
Source: *comment@dejanews.com*

including business and commerce, community, government, humanities, law, leisure and recreation, and social sciences, etc. Professional information specialists were hired to organize Galaxy and oversee the classification process. Only pages that have been submitted to Galaxy are listed within the directory. With the search engine, users can search all Web pages referenced by Galaxy on all text, title, or link text matching on any or all search terms. In addition to Web resources, Galaxy may also be used to search the Galaxy pages index, gopher titles, and telnet resources. Galaxy also provides a useful listing of only its directory pages which contain only new items (items which are less than seven days old). Information on Galaxy may be located from its home page at TradeWave Corporation at http://galaxy.tradewave.com/galaxy.html. (see Figure 2.19).

i-Explorer i-Explorer is a search engine that provides access to sites that have been submitted to its database. Information in i-Explorer is organized into twenty-one broad categories, such as art, classifieds, games, hobbies, news, real estate, and travel. Each category has a number of sub-categories. New items are added to the database when a user submits his site; that user decides which category and sub-

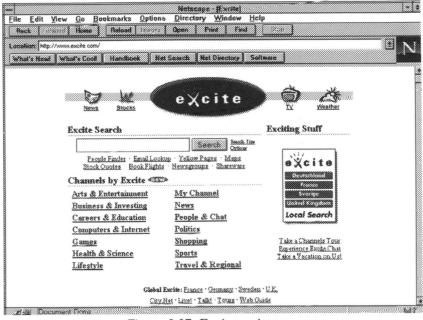

Figure 2.17 Excite main page.

Source: *online form*

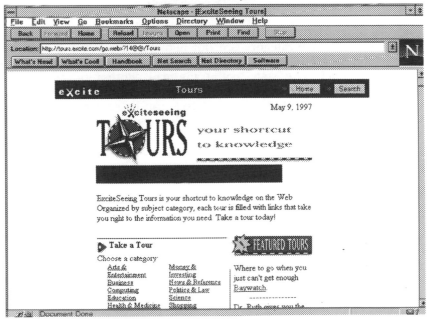

Figure 2.18 Excite tours page.

Source: *online form*

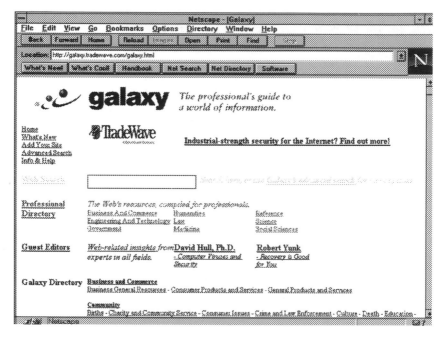

Figure 2.19 Galaxy main page.
Source: *galaxy@tradewave.com*

category is appropriate for the new submission. Duplicate submissions within the same sub-category are not allowed. Users can search for information by site type, whole word, keywords in the document title, description, URL, city, state, country, e-mail address, or submission date. Additionally, users can sort by category, title, description, URL, city, state, or country. The entire database can be searched only from the opening page. Once a category or sub-category has been selected, searches will be executed only within that category or sub-category. More information on i-Explorer may be located from the pages at Online Designs, Inc. at http://www.i-explorer.com/home.dll.

Infoseek Infoseek is another search engine offering both search and directory services. It offers two services, one for the majority of searchers and one for power searchers. The search service for the majority of users responds to natural language queries in English (several other languages are also available) without requiring the use of complex query languages or complex syntax. Power users can also take advantage of more complex structured queries and other advanced features in their searching. Infoseek indexes all words on a page, allows precise searching on proper names, permits searching by symbols and numbers,

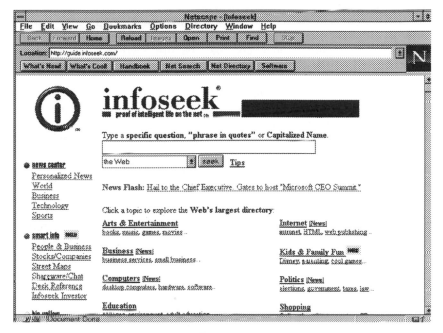

Figure 2.20 Infoseek main page.
Source: *commens@infoseek.com*

Reprinted by permission. Infoseek, the Infoseek logos, 'proof of intelligent life on the net,' Ultraseek, Ultrashop and Ultrasmart are trademarks of Infoseek Corporation which may be registered in certain jurisdictions. Copyright (©) 1995, 1996 Infoseek Cororation.

and permits searching by phrase. Billing itself as the 'Web's largest directory,' Infoseek's directory is a listing of Web sites divided into twelve broad categories including arts, business, computers, entertainment, news, sports, and travel. Information on Infoseek may be located through the Infoseek home page at Infoseek Corporation at http://guide.infoseek.com/ (see Figure 2.20).

Lycos The search engine Lycos was created by Carnegie Mellon University and subsequently spun off for further development through Lycos, Inc. It is one of the more popular and better known search engines. With Lycos, users may search the Web in general or specify a search by pictures, sound, or subject. Subject browsing is provided in sixteen broad categories, including arts/humanities, business/finance, computers, education, Internet, shopping, and the world. Additionally, Lycos has developed some specialized auxiliary information services, such as a current news service in a variety of areas (e.g., world news, business, sports), guides to hundreds of cities throughout the US, stock quotes, and a directory service for finding personal phone numbers and addresses. Information on Lycos may be obtained from its welcome page located on the World Wide Web at http://www.lycos.com/

Magellan   Magellan is an online Internet guide and search engine. The Internet guide contains a directory of rated and reviewed Internet sites as well as a database of sites awaiting review. Sites are rated on depth (comprehensiveness and timeliness), ease of use, and 'net appeal.' Magellan includes Web sites, FTP and gopher servers, newsgroups, and telnet sites in its database and searches. Magellan offers a browse capability within its database through a directory and sub-directory hierarchy which is divided into 26 broad categories including arts, communications, daily living, entertainment, environment, food, mathematics, music, spirituality, and technology. Searches may be limited to only the rated and reviewed database or can include the entire database. Additionally, on many pages searches can be limited to 'green light' sites only. Green light sights are those database sites which, in the review process, were determined to contain no content intended for adult audiences. Magellan has been translated into French and German, and will later be available in other languages. Additional information on Magellan may be on the World Wide Web at http://www.mckinley.com/

Open Text Index   Open Text Index is a search engine with two options: simple search and power search. The simple search option is a single output field that which allows users to enter a group of words or single phrase without further qualification. This is similar to many other search engines. The power search option allows users to choose where in Web pages they want to search for words and phrases. For example, a user can specify that he wants to search everywhere in Web pages or to limit the search by summary, title, first heading, or URL. In addition, the power search option allows the use of proximity operators (and, or, but not, near, or followed by) to combine words and phrases in multiple data entry fields, each of which can be limited as described above. Open Text Index is currently available in several languages, including Japanese, Portuguese, and Spanish. As do many of the other services described here, Open Text Index offers additional specialized search services including searching current events from a variety of newspapers, searching newsgroup postings (using Deja News described above), and e-mail address locators. It also offers several lists of about ten to twelve selections within a variety of categories such as cartoons, columnists, and cool sites. Information on Open Text Index may be located on the World Wide Web at http://index.opentext.net/. (see Figure 2.21).

WebCrawler   WebCrawler is a search engine and directory operated by

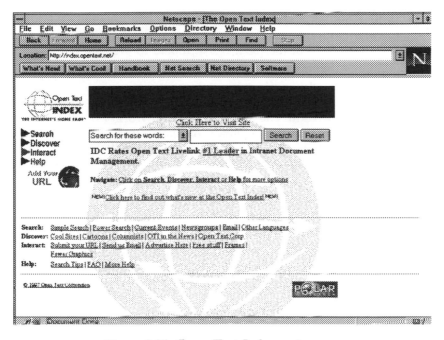

Figure 2.21 Open Text Index main page.
Source: *webmaster@opentext.net*

Excite, Inc. It builds a selective but comprehensive index of the World Wide Web, eliminating combinations of letters and numbers and certain common words, like 'www' or 'web,' from the index to help keep it reasonably small; such words are considered not informative enough in a query. The basic search features search this index using 'natural language searching' of words or phrases in plain English. The advanced feature also offers a range of Boolean operators. Any or all search terms are matched and documents are returned with a ranking indicating how relevant that document is to a user's search. Documents with higher relevance scores appear higher in the list. A browse feature, Web-Crawler Select, provides access to directories and sub-directories of selected 'best' resources, each with a review produced by the Web-Crawler editorial team. The directory is divided into fifteen broad categories, including arts and entertainment, business, computers, daily news, education, humanities, Internet, and personal finance. Among the special features are options to:

- see who has linked to a given Web page;
- to pull up ten random URLs;
- to customize WebCrawler search buttons on your site;

- to find out what topics others are currently searching on Web-Crawler (with the right browser software);
- and to get a list of the top 25 most linked to Web sites.

Information on WebCrawler may be located from its home page at http://www.webcrawler.com/

World Wide Web Worm The World Wide Web Worm (WWWW) is an Internet search engine which builds its index from URLs that are referenced by some other URL already known to WWWW. Therefore, unless a URL is referenced somewhere else, it will not be known to WWWW. Four types of database searches are available:

- citation hypertext (URL references);
- citation addresses (URL addresses);
- HTML document titles, and HTML document addresses.

A database is searched by keyword with options for matching all keywords or any keywords. Information on the World Wide Web Worm may be located at the home page at http://wwww.cs.colorado.edu/wwww.

Yahoo! Yahoo! is probably the most popular and best known Internet resource. Undoubtedly, some of its fame is due to its name. Yahoo! is not a search engine; it is a database of links to Web and Internet resources organized as a hierarchical subject-oriented guide, commonly known as a catalog or directory. Potential new sites (usually submitted by a user) are subsequently added (or 'cataloged') manually by staff who review them and categorize them within the existing classification scheme. Yahoo!'s search facility searches only within the database itself rather than the larger Web. The search engine Alta Vista will search the Web when a search of Yahoo's categories and sites fails to produce a match. Yahoo! is divided into fourteen broad subject categories, including arts, business and economy, education, government, health, reference, and science. Yahoo! includes categories for new and 'cool' sites, and includes a section 'Just Launched on the Web' to publicize new Web sites. The feature 'My Yahoo!' allows users to create their own personal Yahoo! guide to favorite sites and topics of interest. Additionally, Yahoo! is developing regional guides for some communities (New York City, San Francisco Bay, Los Angeles) as well as local guides for some other countries (France, Germany, Japan) in their respective languages. Information on Yahoo! may be located through the home page at http://www.yahoo.com/ (see Figures 2.22–2.23.)

Robots, harvesters, spiders, and Web crawlers

The terms 'robot,' 'harvester,' 'spider,' and 'web crawler' are different ways of referring to programs that are used to roam the Web and index

Figure 2.22 Yahoo! main page.
Source: *online form*
Text and artwork copywrite 1996 by Yahoo!, INC. YAHOO! and the YAHOO!
logo are trademarks of YAHOO! INC.

sites. Web browsers are operated by humans and do not automatically
retrieve referenced documents, and are not robots. As the Web grew,
it became much more difficult to index manually. 'When the size of the
Web increased beyond a few sites and a small number of documents, it
became clear that manual browsing through a significant portion of the
hypertext structure is no longer possible, let alone an effective method
for resource discovery' (Koster, 1995). This led to experimental programs, often called 'robots.' Web robots are programs that search the
Web's hypertext structure and retrieve documents then continue to
retrieve all documents referenced in a given document. While the term
robot may lead us to believe that they are devices which roam the Web
and are capable of some type of movement, a robot is a single software
program that retrieves remote information using Web protocols. Robots
can be used to perform a variety of functions, including:

- statistical analysis (i.e., they can discover and count the number of
  Web servers, count the average number of documents per server,
  or the average size of a Web page)

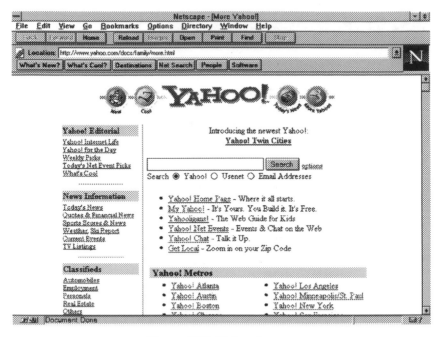

Figure 2.23 Yahoo! pages.
Source: *online form*
Text and artwork copywrite 1996 by Yahoo!, INC. YAHOO! and the YAHOO!
logo are trademarks of YAHOO! INC.

- maintenance (i.e., they can verify links and assist in locating dead links)
- mirroring (i.e., robots are capable of retrieving a sub-tree of Web pages and storing it locally)
- resource discovery (i.e., robots can locate information and summarize large parts of the Web, and provide access to these results through a search engine

(Koster, 1995).

The fourth function, resource discovery, is used by search engines such as ALIWEB, Alta Vista, Excite, Infoseek, and Lycos to build their databases.

Different strategies are used to determine how robots decide which sites to visit. The most common strategy is to start from a historical list of URLs, particularly documents with many links to other sites, such as server lists, 'what's new' pages, and the most popular Web sites (Koster, 1996). A number of indexing services allow individuals to manually submit their URLs, and their sites are later visited by the service's robot. Search engines and companies that use robots are often very upfront about the fact that a robot will later visit sites that want to be linked to the search engine. Robots index different parts of Web documents. For example, some index HTML titles or introductory paragraphs, while others parse META tags or other hidden tags. The manner in which a robot indexes sites has an impact on the success of a user's search and retrieval efforts. Search and retrieval using Web search engines often provide large, unwieldy results or irrelevant citations. Searches produced by using the Web are often far less accurate than those produced by using print indexes or online databases. Indexing produced by robots lacks the ability to differentiate and distinguish between word meanings, phrases, or nuances that are easily distinguished by humans.

While robots perform many useful functions, a growing number of Web managers want to keep them out of their sites. There are various reasons for this, the most obvious being network overload. 'Depending on the frequency with which it requests documents from the server, this can result in a considerable load, which results in a lower level of service for other Web users accessing the server' (Koster, 1995). Robots may prevent individuals from accessing a site. Managers of sites containing volatile or quickly changing information, or of sites under development may also wish to keep robots out (Carl, 1995). The information contained in a newspaper site, for example, can change very often, and if visited by a robot, is likely to produce a dead or useless link by the time it is entered at the site link. Additionally, Koster (1995) points out that the Internet has traditionally been viewed as free, yet this perception is coming under scrutiny by corporations who believe that providing free searches to potential customers are one thing while automated transfers by robots are not.

Felt and Scales (1996) note that since each robot is programmed to search the Web differently, the information stored in each database may vary greatly. A number of search engines including ALIWEB, Alta Vista, Excite, Harvest, HotBot, Infoseek, Inktomi, Lycos, Magellan, Open Text Index, and WebCrawler rely on robots for indexing.

Applications and analysis
The idea of the Internet as a utopia for one-stop shopping is a popular one for many people. A lack of consistency between documents in terms of content, quality, and currency work against those who attempt to make the Internet their sole source of information, as an increasing number of individuals are trying to do. The Internet, and more specifically the Web, have spawned a number of amateur publishers. These sites and documents are frequently not governed by the same standards as many long-standing print publications. The lack of controlled language makes it difficult to search Web documents in the same manner.

The controlled index terms used to search print indexes and LISs do not easily translate into Web searching and provide disappointing results. Unfortunately, the availability, ease of use, and lure of appearance have too many users relying solely on Internet documents to meet their information needs whether or not the documents they retrieve can appropriately meet those needs. Expectations have been raised, and many users believe all the information they need will be available online. This belief is often accompanied by the general feeling that information online is the best and the most current available. While this is often not necessarily the case, many users will stop a search when the Internet fails to yield the desired search results without considering non-Net based resources.

Lanier and Wilkins mention the instability of information on the Internet as new files, databases, etc., are regularly added. Stability of information on the Internet is affected by attrition as resources are removed from the Internet, or access to them is restricted. Information is often not updated regularly as site managers change or leave, or as interest in maintaining the site fades. Although what Lanier and Wilkins (1994) wrote in 1994 still holds true to some extent, efforts have been undertaken to provide order to information available on the Internet. Electronic journals are now indexed in standard print indexes, for example. Many discussion lists and electronic journals have developed comprehensive online archives which are easily accessible to users. Resources have been committed and tools developed to address the long-term archiving needs and related issues surrounding electronic resources.

Internet resource guides and directories and search engines are assisting professionals in accessing the wealth of Internet resources and in providing information to patrons. Internet resource guides, such as the Argus Clearinghouse guides, are helpful in providing information on a given topic. Morville (1996b) describes the characteristics of a good Internet resource guide that contribute to its usability:

- high quality resource entries;
- useful descriptive and evaluative information;
- hypertext links directly to the resources.

Internet directories or catalogs, such as Yahoo!, provide an organizational scheme to facilitate browsing. Directory managers create the top level of organization, and almost anyone can submit information to the directory. The strength of Internet resources lies in their ability to be comprehensive and current (Morville, Rosenfeld, and Janes, 1996, p. 96). In contrast, directories lack editorial control over content and organization. The volume of information makes it impossible for directory managers to review each resource.

Search engines help to create order in the vast resources contained on the Internet, and are useful when conducting extensive research into a particular topic (Morville, Rosenfeld, and Janes, 1996, p. 120). The most comprehensive Internet searches are made possible with search engines, but a basic weakness is their dependence on automated procedures for indexing, organizing, and presenting information. Although recall may be high, precision is often low. A search may produce numerous results, but those results may have very little or no relevance to the search topic. This is in part due to the lack of controlled indexing vocabulary.

Lanier and Wilkins (1994, p. 364) see the Internet as having great potential for providing answers to reference questions. Many standard reference works (encyclopedias, dictionaries, or the *CIA World Fact Book*, for example) now have online versions which can easily be consulted. The advent of technology, particularly Web browsers and hypertext, has made it just as easy to consult information sources outside the library as it is to use a library's collection. Reference service incorporating Internet use is a value added service since the variety of resources potentially available means that fewer users will be turned away from the reference desk empty handed. Lanier and Wilkins stated that the Internet 'is not likely to become a "one-stop shop" for all ready reference queries' (1994, p. 364). Nor can we expect it to be so, just as no single print work, or library's entire collection, can serve all the information needs of its user community. Hence, interlibrary loan arrangements and consortia with reciprocal borrowing agreements came into being. The Internet will meet certain information needs and will cater more to certain audiences. It will co-exist with, rather than supersede or replace, other library resources. When libraries first began considering making electronic resources available to users, the issue of access versus ownership was an obstacle. That has become a dead issue since the emergence of the Web and the variety of resources to which it provides links.

Libraries have reached the conclusion (and have come to terms with the idea) that it is not possible or even realistic for one library to attempt to purchase and own all materials and information relevant to the library's mission. Libraries have traditionally relied on resource sharing to enhance collections. Widespread availability of, and ease of access to, online resources have led many libraries to reap the benefits provided by networked and Internet resources. The bottom line is that access is available to the necessary resources. Owning these resources loses importance as ready access to them is provided through LISs, links on Web pages, and Web browsers.

Budgeting staff time is an important consideration as electronic resources are introduced as a regular part of reference service. Using electronic resources requires familiarity and practice. Libraries must establish policies determining how much time should be devoted to answering reference questions using electronic resources, particularly the Internet (Lanier and Wilkins, 1994, p. 365). The amount of on-the-job time professionals devote to keeping current with Internet resources should also be firmly established. Additionally, libraries need to examine how much material is appropriate to answer a given query. Several print sources may adequately answer a question, yet not all of them will be used. They merely represent the possibilities. The same holds true for Internet resources. Lastly, Lanier and Wilkins stress that professionals, must focus on when to use Internet resources for reference: 'Much of the current interest in the Internet focuses on *how* to use it. Librarians also need to be concerned with *when* to use it' (1994, p. 366).

Chapter 3

Electronic Publishing and Document Delivery Services

Electronic Publishing

Electronic publishing has led to new opportunities to deliver information. In many cases, it has created opportunities for writers who otherwise might not get their work exposed to a wide audience, or who might not gain the chance to publish through the traditional channels provided by mainstream print publishing. Journals have been published electronically since the beginning of the 1990s, yet only recently have publishers begun to make books available electronically. A number of electronic publishers have emerged; plus well known publishers of print materials, including Oxford University Press and Princeton University Press, have started to experiment with electronic publishing. Electronic publishing creates opportunities for users as well as authors and publishers. Many of the electronic books or electronic publishers' Web sites freely permit and encourage readers to provide feedback on works, often directly to the author rather than to the publisher. This chapter will explore electronic publishing projects and electronic journals.

Electronic delivery of information is not limited to books and journals. Document delivery services are helping to make access to information in articles, papers, etc. easier and more convenient for end-users. There is a growing trend for vendors to work directly with patrons, without any involving the library. Users may establish their own accounts, charge services to credit cards or pay by a prearranged method, and have requested materials delivered directly to them by fax, e-mail, etc. This chapter will also discuss some document delivery services and modes of delivery.

Electronic books

McCarty (1997) outlines examples of electronic books and monographs:

- edited books appearing online for the first time, such as Perry Willett's *Victorian Women Writers Project*;
- re-edited books based on print editions, such as Ian Lancashire's project *Representative poetry*, a collection of about 730 poems by about 80 poets, ranging from Wyatt to Swinburne;
- postprints by authors, which are online re-issues of books previously published in print and for which the author still holds the copyright (examples include *Cassidorous* by James J. O'Donnell);
- postprints by editors which include items faithfully reproduced as possibly without significant re-editing of the texts (examples include Columbia University's *Project Bartelby*).

Electronic books also include versions which are available simultaneously in print and on the Web, and books distributed on CD-ROM or floppy disk. While electronic books have not been fully accepted by either readers or publishers, they do provide benefits not possible with their print counterparts. Some of the drawbacks to electronic books are that they are difficult to use for sustained reading from a computer screen, and special equipment is needed to access the book. In contrast, the advantages to using electronic books include 24 hour availability (no need to wait for a library to open; or to place a request if the book has been checked out), it can be accessed from anywhere; it cannot be lost, stolen, or checked out; and copies may be printed on demand (Mitchell, 1996). Additionally, Crawford and Gorman (1995, pp. 17–18) feel that paper and print still work best for sustained reading while electronic distribution of information is better for communicating data and small packets of information.

Despite the fact that more mainstream and scholarly publishers are making books available online, they are still taking precautions to guarantee sales. William Mitchell (1996), author of *City of bits: space, place, and the infobahn*, feels that since publishers have not begun to guarantee the stability of Web sites it is necessary to continue to make print copies available to assure continued access to a title. Concerns have been raised regarding electronic books, since a great deal of effort is required to maintain and update them. Lastly, Mitchell (1996) stresses that considerations should also include how long a book should be made available online, responsibility for long-term archiving, and examination of the electronic equivalent of out of print.

Electronic book projects
This section discusses Michael Hart's *History and philosophy of Project Gutenberg* (1995), William J. Mitchell's *City of bits: space, place and the infobahn* (1995), Mike Franks' *Internet publishing handbook for World Wide Web, gopher, and WAIS* (1995), and projects undertaken by Princeton University Press.

Project Gutenberg Project Gutenberg's goal is to make texts available in the simplest and easiest to use forms at an affordable price (Dell, 1995). Texts are made available in ASCII, and the Project has been releasing four high quality electronic texts per month into the public domain since 1991. Texts are available by ftp at mrcnext.cso.uiuc.edu in the /extext subdirectory. Gutenberg texts are divided into three portions:

- 'light' literature such as *Alice in Wonderland, Aesop's Fables*, and *Peter Pan*;
- 'heavy' literature such as the Bible, Shakespeare's works, and *Moby Dick*;
- reference works such as *Roget's Thesaurus* and almanacs, encyclopedias, and dictionaries.

Additional information on Project Gutenberg is available on the Web at http://www.promo.net/pg/. An index of Project Gutenberg texts is available at http://www.promo.net/pg/lists/list.html.

City of Bits: Space, Place, and the Infobahn Author William J. Mitchell believes that his book may be the first to be made available simultaneously in print as well as in full-text on the Web. Often, publishers will make a synopsis or summary, or the table of contents of a print edition of a book available on the Web to entice readers to buy it. Making a book available in different versions is not a new idea; publishers often do this with more expensive hardbacks and lesser priced paperbacks. Mitchell found that making his book available on the Web actually led to widescale reading and reviewing in some countries before the print version was available.

A number of things were done to provide a connection between the print and Web versions of the book. For example the online version provided a link to an order from which could be used for ordering the print version. In turn, the URL for the Web version appeared on the dust jacket of the print version. While many publishers are reluctant to make potentially profitable items available for free on the Web, Mitchell and MIT Press felt that this risk would be offset by the sales generated by the Web site. Their hunch was correct and about 2% of sales for the book's first printing were from the online order form (Mitchell, 1996). They believe the Web site may also have helped to drive bookstore and mail order sales.

One unique feature of the book is that it includes an online 'agora' where readers can post their comments, which may be read by others, including the author. Readers can also add links to sites which they feel are relevant and appropriate. In addition, the author will occasionally contribute to the discussion. Lastly, in lieu of an index, the book offers an internal search engine which permits keyword searching. Endnotes are available by a clickable link to the note, which is a feature quite common to Web documents.

Different strategies were used to generate publicity for the online version of the book, including providing a link from MIT press' online catalog to the book. The online version has a welcome page that provides links to a synopsis, Mitchell's home page, and the book's table of contents. Links from other sites also facilitated access to the book. The book may be accessed on the World Wide Web on the MIT Press home page at http://www-mitpress.mit.edu/City_of_Bits/.

Two similar projects follow.

The Internet publishing handbook: for World Wide Web, gopher, and WAIS Mike Franks has also written a book which is available both in print and in full-text on the Web. The Web version provides separate pages for publication data, dedication information, acknowledgments, notes on differences between the print and HTML versions, and a collection of Internet links to topics, sites, etc. cited in the text. As with *City of bits: space, place, and the infobahn*, readers may e-mail the author with comments and feedback on the book. Franks' book is located on the World Wide Web at http://www.sscnet.ucla.edu/ssc/franks/book/.

Princeton University Press Princeton University Press currently has 3 books available on the Web: *Trapped in the Net* by Gene I. Rochlin, *Making the modern reader* by Barbara M. Benedict, and *Gender and immortality* by Deborah Lyons. Each book has its own page including a description of the book, the complete table of contents, and full-text of the book. The books also include a search page at the end following the bibliography, which permits keyword and Boolean searching. Unlike Mitchell and Franks' books, links are not provided so that readers may contact the authors, nor are there links to other relevant sites. Additionally, these books are also available in print, and are included in Princeton University Press' online book catalog. More information on Princeton's Books Online is available at http://pup.princeton.edu/books/.

Electronic Publishers

BookWire This publisher provides information on electronic books (fiction, nonfiction/reference, and children's books), including background information on authors and an index to author Web sites. BookWire also provides authors, publicists, and marketers with an opportunity to publicize and market works. This site also provides links to the online literary magazine *Bold Type, Publishers Weekly,* and to

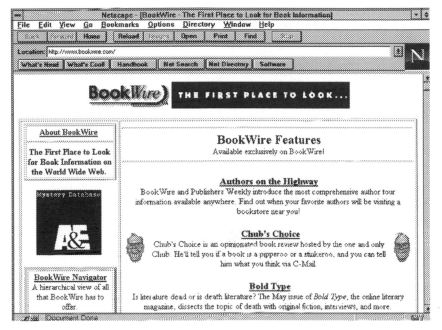

Figure 3.1 Book Wire main page.
Source: *www@bookwire.com*

the industry newsletter *Subtext*, in addition to numerous other links. The BookWire Reading Room provides direct links to electronic texts in the public domain, and entire texts may be downloaded by readers. Further information on BookWire is available on the Web at http://www.bookwire.com/ (see Figure 3.1.).

Digital Library The Digital Library (DL) is an online electronic library that provides access to nonfiction, poetry, and short fiction. The service is currently free to test the demand for this type of library. The DL actively solicits submissions, providing new authors with an opportunity to gain exposure for their work. Links are available so that readers can directly e-mail authors to comment on their work. A short blurb is included about each author. The DL also features a section on Internet literary resources which includes information on Beat poets and personalities, the literary magazine *The Word*, and the complete works of Shakespeare in a searchable annotated and indexed format. More information on the DL is available on the World Wide Web at http://www.c2.org/~library/.

Eastgate Systems Eastgate Systems is a publisher which solicits hyper-

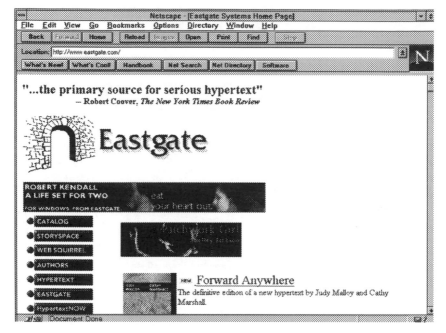

Figure 3.2 Eastgate Systems Home pages.
Source: *info@eastgate.com*

text (fiction and nonfiction), and provides Storyspace, a hypertext writing environment (Eastgate Systems, Inc., 1996). This format is best suited for working with large and complex hypertexts, and allows authors to create texts which they are free to distribute without royalty. Storyspace hypertext can be saved as a stand-alone program, or exported to the Web. A list of sites developed or maintained using Storyspace is available at http://www.eastgate.com/Hypertext.html. The Eastgate site also provides a catalog of hypertext publications and books, and a page featuring author information (including photographs of the authors). Additional information on Eastgate Systems is available on the Web at the publisher's home page at http://www.eastgate.com/. (see Figure 3.2.).

Electronic Book Aisle The Electronic Book Aisle (EBA) bills itself as 'The Web's premiere site for fully-searchable electronic books' (OverDrive Systems, Inc., 1996). EBA is a searchable interactive catalog of electronic books, and users can view book covers, jackets, author profiles, or tables of contents. This site primarily features fiction, non-fiction, reference, self-help, and how-to books. Hypertext links are

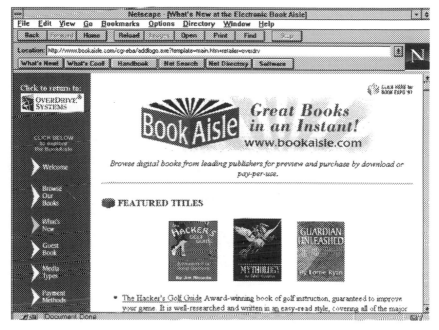

Figure 3.3 Electronic Book Aisle main page.
Source: *publishing@bookaisle.com*

provided to related topics, and the site includes links to retailers who use EBA's services. Displays include the complete text of books and illustrations, and a free download is available weekly from EBA. Users can purchase an entire book with a viewer for download, or choose pay-per-view access to selected sections of a book. Different options are available to purchase books from EBA:

- through download to Windows-compatible PCs;
- books may be viewed using standard Web browsers;
- some titles are available on CD-ROM or floppy disk;
- print editions may be ordered. Visit the Electronic Book Aisle on the World Wide Web at http://www.bookaisle.com/. (see Figure 3.3.).

Yahoo! Yahoo! provides a section on Web published fiction. 'Published' in this context is quite different from the traditional print publication process. In this case, the act of making these works available on the Web makes them 'published.' Works include images as well as text. Links to characters, author information, etc. are available. Authors may

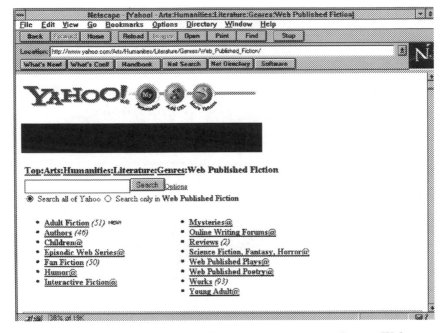

Figure 3.4 Yahoo! Top:Arts:Humanities:Literature:Genres:Web.
Published Fiction:Works main page
Source: *webmaster@yahoo.com*
Text and artwork copywrite 1996 by Yahoo!, INC. YAHOO! and the YAHOO!
logo are trademarks of YAHOO! INC.

be e-mailed in some cases. Style and content vary greatly between each
story. This site is located on the World Wide Web at http://www.yahoo.com/
Recreation/Games/Interactive—Fiction/ (see Figure 3.4.).

Alive and Free Alive and Free is a page of links to recent free online
literature from living authors including fiction and nonfiction, and books
and excerpts from books. This page is located on the Web at http://
www.c3f.com/alivfree.html.

Electronic Journals

Electronic publishing has led to a new era of communications and
information sharing. Electronic journals have helped publishers and scholars to disseminate information much more quickly than was previously
possible. Initially, electronic journals were seen by many as a passing

fad. Many in the library profession considered them problematic and inappropriate for library collections since they presented problems in terms of acquisitions, subscriptions, cataloging, and archiving. Automating journals was a logical progression of the trend in libraries to automate routine practices such as cataloging and circulation. The emergence of electronic journals followed the widespread adoption and use of electronic mail, listservs and discussion groups to disseminate information quickly to large audiences. Franks (1993a) offers several reasons why electronic publishing was adopted by scholarly research journals long before it was used for other kinds of publications:

- the intended audience uses the Internet more than the general population and is familiar with using documents in an electronic form;
- libraries are experiencing extreme financial hardship and cutbacks in funding;
- there is a strong move for scholars to find less costly ways to promote their work.

Although Franks' reasoning is valid and continues to hold true, electronic journals have not become as central to scholarly publishing and libraries as some forward thinking individuals might have anticipated. A discussion of this issue is included in the next section.

Characteristics of electronic journals

The term 'electronic journal' is ambiguous, and it is not always clear whether the producers of a given title are referring to a distribution format for a print journal, an electronic archive of a print journal, or a journal published exclusively in an electronic format (Covi, 1996). Electronic journals come in a variety of styles and formats, much like their print counterparts. Early electronic journals were primitive with unattractive layouts, and were difficult to read. They frequently lacked page numbers, making it difficult to navigate the text or to refer to portions of it. Some journals attempted to solve this problem by including line numbers at various points throughout the journal (such as at the beginning of a new article or section). Surprisingly, a number of electronic journals continue to use this practice. Users of early electronic journals often printed hard copies, and many libraries preferred to provide paper printouts of the electronic journal rather than access to the actual online version.

Duranceau *et al.* (1996) describe early and contemporary versions of electronic journals as 'first-generation' and 'second-generation' electronic journals. Each generation shares a set of common characteristics. First-generation electronic journals often are:

- ASCII-text files;

- simple file structures (one file equals one article, or one file equals one issue);
- published by individuals or groups of scholars;
- disseminated by e-mail, and the implied audience is the individual subscriber;
- copyright restrictions are usually waived to the extent that proper attribution is made.

(Duranceau *et al.*, 1996, p. 49)

Second-generation electronic journals are often:

- HTML-based or use the Web to disseminate specially formatted issues;
- issues or articles include graphics, multimedia, or links to other Internet resources;
- file structures are less hierarchical, and there is less uniformity in structure from one title to another
- users are notified by e-mail when new issues are available, and may retrieve issues from the server.

(Duranceau *et al.*, 1996, p. 50)

Electronic journals have undergone a dramatic transformation in style and format since their initial appearance in the early 1990s. Many now have full-color Web pages with an attractive and easy to use layout. Despite the fact that layout and presentation of electronic journals have greatly improved, and access has been facilitated by the Web and online archives, users still may prefer to print hard copies of selected issues and articles to reading from a computer screen.

Some of the more common distribution methods include (PICK, 1996):

1. electronic journals available through Internet applications Described as the 'classic electronic journal,' this is the format with which most of us are familiar, and is how the majority of users define an electronic journal. *LIBRES: Library and Information Science Research Electronic Journal, McJournal: The Journal of Academic Media Librarianship, PACS Review*, and *The Olive Tree: A Library and Information Sciences Electronic Journal* exemplify this type of electronic journal. The first three titles originally were distributed via e-mail, but are now available on the Web. For this reason, only announcements of new issues are distributed by e-mail or to listservs. In contrast, *The Olive Tree* was available exclusively on the Web, a first for an electronic journal, but it has now ceased publication. *LIBRES, McJournal*, and the *PACS Review* are first generation electronic journals which have evolved into second generation electronic journals. Subscriptions and access to this category of electronic journal are free.

2. print journals and parallel publications These journals are published simultaneously in print and electronically. The online version may include the full-text of the journal, only the table of contents, or selected articles and excerpts from the print version. Well known popular publications such as *Time* (http://pathfinder.com/@@PIK7awQAh7xEqAOX/time/) and *U.S News and World Report* (http://www.usnews.com/) and *Scientific American* (http://www.sciam.com/) now have Web sites that offer previews and excerpts of issues. For obvious reasons, the electronic version is always available much more quickly than its print counterpart. It is safe to assume that electronic journals in this category are second generation.

Franks (1993a) describes two other types of electronic journals: the database model and the software model. Under the database model, articles reside in a centralized database maintained by the publisher. The service is similar to Lexis/Nexis and DIALOG, and subscribers are given permission to access the database and use search software on the central computer to locate and download articles. With the software model, a subscriber gets a piece of software which runs on an Internet connected computer and connects to the database of the journal's central computer (Franks, 1993a). The user can search and download information which will be sent in a proprietary encrypted form. The software would have an expiration date that corresponds with the length of the subscription.

Commercial publishers have also made journal titles available on CD-ROM. These are considered by many as electronic journals. The full-text of such journals as the *Economist, New Scientist*, the *Journal of the American Medical Association*, and newspapers such as *Le Monde* and the *Washington Post* have been made available on CD-ROM (Woodward and McKnight, 1995, p. 72). In many cases, these titles duplicate print titles already held by libraries. Libraries have often subscribed to journals both in print and on microform. This is a continuation of that idea and supplement the library's collection.

Planning for access
While print journals have traditionally presented problems for libraries, electronic journals have defied traditional acquisitions, collection development, cataloging, and public services practices. Libraries are divided over whether or not to include bibliographic records for electronic journals easily accessible through an individual subscription or via the Web in their LISs. Some individuals feel the catalog should represent only those things acquired and owned by the library. Others, such as Eric Lease Morgan, creator of the Index Morganagus program for cataloging electronic journals, see the LIS as a finding aid to resources both within and beyond the library. To these individuals, the LIS no longer solely represents physical items located on-site, and

ownership versus access is no longer an issue. For those who have decided to catalog electronic journals, the question of how to catalog and best represent electronic journals continues to present problems. Librarians find it difficult to create a bibliographic record for something that lacks a physical form and location. Many libraries would like to provide hypertext links from bibliographic records in their LISs, if their local systems could provide for this capability. One solution is to provide notes in the bibliographic record providing details on how to access a title or instructing users to inquire at the reference desk for assistance.

At some libraries, LISs have been superseded by Web pages for providing access to electronic journals. It is becoming less common for LISs to contain bibliographic records for electronic journals, particularly for titles available via the Internet or through consortial agreements, such as the Committee on Institutional Cooperation's Electronic Journals Collection (CIC-EJC). Libraries often include in their LISs only those electronic journals for which there is a paid subscription, such as the *Online Journal of Current Clinical Trials*. The reasons for this are obvious. Libraries believe that something for which there is a fee and demand should be represented in the LIS, as opposed to a title which is free and easily available to anyone with access to the Internet.

It is becoming very common for a library's Web page to include access to the LIS and to provide links to the various electronic journals. Libraries are providing access to selected electronic journals through Web pages, yet not including these titles in the LIS. Web pages are being used to provide what many had initially hoped LISs would which is to provide access to non-owned remotely accessible resources. This solution may be acceptable for more sophisticated users, yet it does not particularly help less experienced users or those with low-end equipment or limited access such as through a dial-up connection or telnet.

Libraries may also opt not to catalog electronic journal titles that duplicate print titles held in their collections, such as electronic titles available through remote hosts such as DIALOG or on CD-ROM. In the case of remote online journals, Woodward and McKnight (1995, p. 72) state that 'Such e-journals are unlikely to be considered part of a library's collection because, in most libraries, users are rarely allowed free and unlimited access to remote online systems. . . .As they are not locally available, online e-journals do not require bibliographic control at a local level.' The choice not to catalog these titles or not to include them in the LIS is a disservice to patrons. While librarians may see them as problematic and difficult to catalog, they are still part of a collection and available resources, and users should be made aware of their existence.

Electronic journals provide archiving problems as well. Libraries must decide whether to provide access to back issues or to maintain local archives. 'The apparently simple matter of whether or not libraries should archive electronic journals turns out to be one of the thorniest issues to be faced in the age of digital media' (Duranceau *et al.*, 1996, p. 47). Questions have been raised concerning the long-term storage implications of electronic journals. Some professionals are convinced that the electronic journal will not gain widespread acceptance with the scholarly community until this issue is resolved. Some of the archiving options currently in use include:

- network-based journals (*Postmodern Culture*, for example) may be acquired from the publisher as offline products, such as fiche or floppy disks;
- publishers of electronic journals maintain archives of backfiles at network sites;
- libraries provide access to back issues through Web pages and gopher sites

(Neavill and Shéble, 1995, p. 14)

Initially, individuals or groups of scholars were the main groups who published electronic journals. Concern has been expressed in the library profession regarding the ability of these groups to provide permanent and reliable archiving. Fortunately, even with changes in editorship, these groups for the most part have done an excellent job of archiving and providing access to back issues. It is much easier to retrieve back issues from a Web site than through a listserv's archives. It also permits users to read the desired articles and decide whether they are applicable before printing them.

Archiving is also being provided by groups like the CIC-EJC which was started in 1992 as an archival project of the Committee on Institutional Cooperation (CIC), an academic consortium of major research libraries. Thirteen member libraries are building and maintaining an archive of electronic serials to be used by member libraries. Access is available for nonmember libraries, and is provided to public domain titles in the archive by gopher servers outside the consortium. This policy may change in the future depending on demands placed on the system.

A number of electronic journals are stored in archives accessible through gopher or the World Wide Web, or in many cases, both. The mode of retrieval for back issues is not limited to obtaining files through ftp since many Web sites provide easy and convenient access through hypertext links. This has solved the archiving issue for many libraries. Initially, some libraries provided access to back issues of electronic journals for a limited period of time, storing the back issues on their local systems or on magnetic tape. It was soon discovered, however, that the implications for storage space and time commitment were overwhelming, and much greater than the typical busy library could easily manage.

Promoting usage of electronic journals is another issue libraries must face. Libraries must decide how they want to advocate use of and publicize electronic journals to their users. Decisions must be made regarding how much user education, if at all, should be provided. Libraries are unsure what to provide (a printout, a file, a URL?) when patrons request articles from electronic journals (Kling and Covi, 1995).

Some electronic serials are often merely electronic versions of print titles that already have bibliographic records. Titles available on non-networked CD-ROMs can cause problems when they are used to replace a large number of print journals. Woodward and McKnight (1995, p. 72) question the usefulness of CD-ROM electronic journal titles:

> In a networked environment, hardware costs . . . systems staff time in implementing and maintaining the CD-ROM network, plus additional network subscription charges can be substantial . . . It may not be premature to question whether CD-ROM networks are the best way to deliver information to the desktops of users.'

Despite some resistance from librarians and logistical problems early on, the electronic journal is here to stay, although it will never supplant the print journal. The two types of journals have coexisted thus far and will continue to do so. Just as microfilm did not eliminate or diminish the need for books, electronic journals will not make print journals obsolete.

Comparison with print journals

Evidence of the stability of electronic journals is reflected by the fact that many are now indexed in standard print sources such as *Library Literature* and *Library and Information Science Abstracts (LISA)*. Although it may seem like an anomaly that an online publication is indexed in a print publication, it reflects the growing acceptance of electronic journals by the library profession and users.

A survey of the literature notes that electronic journals are not fully exploiting the potential advantages of the medium. Some of the innovative features available for use with electronic journals include:

- searchable text;
- hypertext links to other resources;
- use of color graphics, photographs, video, and audio;
- the ability to provide unedited prepublication advance copies of articles.

The authors concluded from their survey results, 'Despite this it is clear that the new "online" medium is not being exploited since many new online journals are simply electronic editions of paper journals' (Hitchcock, Carr, and Hall, 1996).

One of the more obvious advantages which electronic journals have over their print counterparts is speed. Production of an issue of a journal is accomplished much more quickly since communications between the editorial board, reviews of submissions, and exchange of information can proceed much more quickly than through the channels typically used for print journals. The personal computer and the Internet are advantages in electronic publishing. With a personal computer and the Internet, it is now possible for even one person to take full responsibility for the output of a document up to, and including, production of the final copy (Inglis, 1993). Although electronic journals can be produced more quickly than their print counterparts, the editorial work to support a journal published exclusively online can be substantial (Covi, 1996). While the time lag for many processes associated with print publication has been removed, a good deal of time may be spent attracting potential contributors and readers, reviewing and refereeing articles, producing and distributing issues, and maintaining an online archive. Additionally, since electronic journals can reach a wide audience quickly, information can be distributed almost as soon as it is made available, and is stored once it is entered online.

Franks (1993b) suggests that ease of access and quality of user inter-face are important evaluative criteria for electronic journals. How well an electronic journal supports subscribers is also important. It should offer more functionality than a print journal, and copies of articles from an electronic journal should be comparable in quality to a photocopy made from a print journal. 'Simply viewing an article on a computer screen will not be acceptable, nor will a printed copy in a markup language' (Franks, 1993b).

Brent (1995) suggests that print publications provide 'tangible, object-centered quality indicators. Expensively produced, polished-looking journals naturally carry a prestige that cheaply produced journals do not.' An electronic journal that is not substantially better or cheaper than its print counterpart will have limited success (Franks, 1993b). Some of the reasons why scholars shy away from publishing on the Internet include the belief that it is not suitable for serious scholarship; it will generate too much information, making it difficult to locate relevant information in the future; it will eventually cost money, and it cannot ensure archiving in perpetuity (Harnad, 1995a). Furthermore, there is a reluctance on the part of the producers of print journals to move to electronic versions. They feel that moving from a print to an electronic journal will result in a loss of revenues and that their publi-cations will lose prestige since authors are often unwilling to publish in electronic journals. According to Kraft (1993) some areas of concern for scholars and publishers are:

1. costs and acquisitions budgets Can libraries afford to purchase and support both print and electronic versions? Is it practical to purchase electronic versions of a title when the library also owns a complete run in print? Is one format more suitable and more cost effective than another?

2. user friendliness Is the journal easy to use and navigate? Can users read and use it with minimal effort?

3. formatting Will formatting present problems not associated with print journals?

4. access Is access to current issues easy and available in a variety of formats? Is access to back issues readily available?

5. obsolescence Will this format become obsolete with the passing of time? How stable is the publication and what is the scope of coverage?

6. scholarly recognition How will this mode of publication be viewed by peers, colleagues, other scholars? How much weight does an article in a peer reviewed electronic journal carry in comparison to a peer reviewed print journal?

7. attributes of electronic journals, such as reduced production/distribution lead time Lead time for editing and production are greatly reduced. Will quality be sacrificed as a result?

A comparison between three well known and established electronic journals and three widely recognized print journals follows (see Figure 3.5). The electronic journals are *LIBRES: Library and Information Research Electronic Journal, McJournal: The Journal of Academic Media Librarianship*, and *PACS Review.* The print titles are *College and Research Libraries, Information Technology and Libraries*, and the *Journal of Academic Librarianship.*

Upon examination, it is apparent that the three electronic journals are not radically different from their print counterparts. All titles have an ISSN, an editorial board composed of professionals/experts, peer reviewed submissions, and are cited in standard print indexes. Although the electronic journals may not be as widely indexed as their print counterparts, this may be attributed in part to the relative newness of the medium. Additionally, their scope is often much more narrowly defined than that of print journals.

Another difference between the electronic journals and their print counterparts is that for the former information on submissions and retrieval of back issues is often easily available (it typically appears with each issue and is also provided on the journal's Web site). This

Title	ISSN	Editorial Board	Peer Review	Indexing*	Mode of Sub-mission	Mode of Dist./ Retrieval	Turn-around time for pub.
LIBRES	yes	yes	Double blind; at least 2 years	1,2	Email	Listerv, ftp, gopher, Web	Reviews made w/in 45 days
Mc Journal	yes	yes	yes	1	Email, disk	Listerv, Web	Not Given
PACS Review	yes	yes	Double blind	1,3	Email, disk	Listerv, gopher, Web	4–6 weeks
Coll. & Research Libs.	yes	yes	Double blind	1, 2, 4, 5, 9	Paper, disk, email	Postal mail	About 10 months
Info. Tech. & Libs.	yes	yes	Referred	1, 2, 5, 6, 7, 8	Paper, disk (for final version for pub.)	Postal mail	Not given
J. of Acad. Librship	yes	yes	Double blind; at least 3 refs.	1, 2, 4, 5, 6, 9, 10	Paper, disk (for final version for pub.)	Postal mail; OCLC databases	About 6–8 wks. after accept-ance

*1=Library Literature
2=Current Index to Journals in Education
3=ERIC
4=Library and Information Science Abstracts
5=Social Sciences Citation Index

6=Current Contents
7=Magazine Index
8=New Search
9=Information Science Abstracts
10=Education Index

Figure 3.5 Comparison of electronic journals and print scholarly journals

information may appear only in selected issues of the print journals. Electronic journals provide easy access to back issues through hypertext links, and the editors may be e-mailed directly through hot links. Links are also provided for the various modes of access for back issues of the electronic journals.

Submissions to electronic journals are most often made through electronic mail. Submissions to print journals may require several print copies of the manuscript plus a disk. An electronic manuscript can be routed very quickly to reviewers and editors. The time formerly spent sending manuscripts to reviewers and receiving their responses through postal mail is eliminated. With electronic journals and e-mail, editors can receive responses from reviewers almost immediately.

Turnaround time for publication is relatively short for electronic journals (4–6 weeks was the maximum), as compared to 10 months for one of the print publications. Information may well be out of date due to the time lag. All of the journals examined are served by editorial boards that are composed of volunteers, indicating that the motives for participation are the same regardless of format: recognition, prestige, and a desire to contribute to the profession.

Response to electronic journals

Electronic publishing has led to a boom of online publishing by 'self authors,' or 'self-publishers.' Drawbacks to the electronic publishing boom include lack of style and questionable or limited content (particularly when a print counterpart exists). The rash of self-publishing which has been brought about by the Internet and World Wide Web, combined with lack of consistency and quality, has led many to question the validity of all electronic journals. Some individuals feel that anything that one makes available on the Web is 'published.' In the context of this book, 'publications' are comparable to those which are printed – journals, books, position papers, proceedings and essays.

Responses to electronic journals vary greatly. 'Attitudes about publishing and reading electronic journals both shape and are shaped by the technology of electronic journals' (Covi, 1997). Some individuals still view the format as experimental. Individuals involved in the tenure and promotion process may feel that electronic journals are not legitimate or established avenues for publication. Scholars are confused about the formats and intellectual quality of electronic journals. The manner in which electronic journal editors design the format of articles and distribution channels influence acceptability by scholars (Kling and Covi, 1995). Furthermore, the long-term success of an electronic journal requires acceptance by readers, editors, and contributors who help attract readership and respected contributors. This mistrust of electronic journals is based on a lack of understanding of their organizational structure and how they operate. Misconceptions range from fear that anyone can easily tamper with contents to the belief that a journal title will cease publication after interest and novelty have worn off. In reality, there are refereed electronic journals of high quality apparently unknown to the critics. Kling and Covi (1995) describe the scholarly view of electronic journals in this manner,

> Most academics now view electronic publishing as experimental at best. The segregation of electronic journals into an electronic space that isn't [yet] integrated into the scholarly document systems of libraries, indices, abstracting services, and so on is a formula for continued marginality.

This is not completely true since growing public awareness of the Web has increased the acceptance of electronic journals as legitimate publications. Researchers may dislike reading electronic journals from a computer screen, and prefer to print and read the information which they need. Covi (1997) points out that electronic journals are actually more convenient for researchers who value time and searchability, even when the desired information is eventually printed as hard copy.

Supporters of electronic publishing, such as Stevan Harnad, a specialist in electronic communication and advocate of electronic journals, see influence and prestige as the benefits of scholarly publishing. Authors want their work to be made available to a large audience, and like a final say in where it will be published (Franks, 1993a). Electronic journals readily provide scholars with this opportunity. In contrast, Lary (1994) offers the type of criticism that is typically directed at traditional print journals:

> editorial boards accept articles primarily from directors of large (usually university) libraries and most often from library-information graduate faculty; the literature has been dominated by the 'movers and shakers' of ALA; editors help their friends to join the ranks of those publishing.

The flexibility and possibilities offered by electronic journals normally do not involve these types of issues (at least not at this point in time).

The long-term success of electronic journals relies in large part on the support provided by library professionals. Librarians have incentives to support this new role since it preserves their traditional roles as archivers and catalogers, and library budgets can better support archiving electronic journals than the high cost of acquiring print journals (Franks, 1993a). Participation by editors is an important part of establishing an electronic journal's reputation. Notable contributors can help establish a journal's focus and intended audience. A journal's focus should establish its relationship to existing paper and electronic publishing forums (Covi, 1997). The availability of electronic journals through the World Wide Web and easy access to back issues for users, combined with the growing number of online document delivery services geared towards the end-user, have eliminated libraries from the process in many cases. Vendors are making it easy for users to establish their own accounts, and can deliver information to users by fax, postal mail, or the Internet directly to users. In addition, users can get the information they need directly from their own computers in the case of the Web and other modes of Internet access.

Commercial publishers and electronic journals

Commercial publishers have begun to experiment with electronic publishing. Declining print subscriptions and rising publishing costs have made publishers realize that electronic publishing can no longer be regarded as a passing trend. The continuing success of some noncommercial electronic journals has attracted the attention of commercial publishers who are beginning to realize the potential of this format. Woodward and McKnight (1995, p. 76–7) believe that electronic journals cannot ultimately continue to be free since commercial publishers are becoming increasingly involved with electronic publishing, and it is not likely that scholars or libraries can assume responsibility for the dissemination of scholarly information that has traditionally been handled by commercial publishers and learned societies. Additionally, large increases in network traffic, network charges, and the commercialization of the Internet may threaten the tradition of free and open exchange of information.

Electronic publishing poses financial challenges for commercial publishers. The decline in printing publications and the future demand for more electronic services will impact on higher education and research libraries for four reasons:

- For the immediate future the basic formal mechanism for scholarly communication will continue to be books and journals. The distribution medium will gradually change (at least for journals) from paper to electronic.
- When universities are fully equipped to handle electronic information, there will be powerful groups of companies prepared to offer it;
- Electronic services will not be cheaper than print, but they will provide more options and ways to recover costs;
- Service will be a critical factor for success.

(Hunter, 1993, p. 27)

Electronic journals are predominantly distributed in two ways:

- through publishers – titles are offered directly through the Internet which allows the publisher to completely control the process;
- through aggregators – these are intermediate services which offer titles from different publishers through one interface (Machovec, 1997).

Pricing and security are two additional concerns which publishers of electronic journals must handle. First publishers have to solve the issue of trying to recover costs for electronic journals. This is particularly significant for digital documents since they are expensive to maintain and create. Mounting journals on the Web may also lead individuals to cancel paper subscriptions, further reducing the publisher's revenue. This may be solved by making the print copy more attractive by adding extra services and features.

Publishers now offer a variety of pricing structures. These may include offering access to the electronic journal at a reduced cost to the print version. Different subscription costs may also be used for different types of subscribers (individuals, libraries, consortia). Academic Press, for example, offers 176 electronic titles to consortia at ten percent above the print subscription cost. Conversely, publishers may offer free access to an electronic journal if a print subscription is maintained.

Second, publishers must deal with the conflicting desires of offering full access to electronic journals on the Web while maintaining security for subscribers and keeping others out. To solve this problem, publishers often make available free sample issues, articles, or tables of contents. A discussion of selected publishers, aggregators, and electronic journal projects follows.

Electronic journal publishers/aggregators/projects
There are a number of services and projects involving commercial publishers and electronic journals. In this sense, electronic journals have entered the next phase of access. Previously, access was random and spread through word of mouth, or publicized on listservs or the Internet. Publishers are presenting electronic journals as part of a package or service which may include cataloging and often includes archiving. The projects that will be discussed are: Academic Press' IDEAL/APPEAL, ADONIS, the Committee on Institutional Cooperation's Electronic Journal Collection, JSTOR, OCLC's Electronic Journals Online, Project Muse, the Red Sage Project, SuperJournal, and the TULIP project.

Academic Press International Digital Electronic Access Library (IDEAL) is an electronic service that includes the complete 1996 runs of 175 Academic Press journals, as well as some 1995 issues; about 2000 articles are added monthly (Academic Press, 1996). To access IDEAL users need an Internet connection, a Web browser (Netscape or Microsoft Internet Explorer, for example), and an Adobe Acrobat reader. Acrobat is a software product used to manipulate documents stored in Portable Document Format which is 'the file format for representing documents in a manner that is independent of the original application software, hardware and operating system used to create those documents' (Howe, 1996). Journals available through IDEAL include those in the biomedical sciences, engineering and material sciences, life sciences, psychology, and social sciences.

Academic Press Print and Electronic Access (APPEAL), is a site license for large consortia, providing access at sites within a consortium to journal titles formerly held in print locations anywhere within the consortium. In 1995, Academic Press signed an APPEAL agreement with 180 British colleges and universities. Agreements were signed with consortia in North America, Europe, and the Far East the following year. Information on IDEAL and APPEAL may be found on the Web at http://www.apnet.com/www/ap/aboutid.htm.

IDEAL and APPEAL are part of a three-year project undertaken by Academic Press to use the Internet to provide access to scientific journals which are delivered directly to the user's desktop. Mirror sites are maintained in the United States at http://www.idealibrary.com and in the United Kingdom at http://www.europe.idealibrary.com. Available journal issues are maintained at two sites: http://www.apnet.com/www/ap/whatsnew.htm or http://www.europe.apnet.com/www/ap/whatsnew.htm. The APPEAL site license is available at http://www.apnet.com/www/ap/genlay.htm.

ADONIS ADONIS Electronic Journal Subscriptions (EJS) is a service that began in 1997, providing subscribers with only the titles which they choose. Subscribers receive electronic journal titles concurrently at prices comparable to the print version. About 400 titles are currently available, and more are being added. Special archival CD-ROMs are available to consolidate the electronic journal titles. The service also provides full bibliographic indexes that include abstract and keyword searching. Further information on EJS may be found on the World Wide Web at http://www.adonis.nl/ddeses.htm.

The Committee on Institutional Cooperation's Electronic Journals Collection (CIC-EJC) The CIC-EJC is a collection of electronic journals provided to member libraries of the Committee on Institutional Cooperation (CIC), the academic consortium of members of the Big Ten athletic conference and the University of Chicago. CIC-EJC serves as the electronic journal collection for member libraries, incorporating all freely distributed journals available online (Committee on Institutional Cooperation, 1996a). The collection has been cataloged by member libraries and bibliographic records are included in the OCLC online database. Interestingly, CIC institutions do not include bibliographic records for these titles in their LISs (with a few minor exceptions, such as *Current Cites* and *Psyqoloquy* in the case of one library). One of the goals of the CIC-EJC is to create a single master database of bibliographic records for titles in the collection, making it possible for one person to maintain the collection (Committee on Institutional Cooperation, 1996b). Information on CIC-EJC is available on the World Wide Web at http://ejournals.cic.net/.

JSTOR JSTOR was originally conceived by William G. Bowen, President of the Mellon Foundation, as a solution for libraries that lacked adequate space to store back issues of scholarly journals. His plan was to convert back issues to an electronic format to save space and money and to improve access to back issues thus finding a solution to preser-

vation issues associated with storing print copies of journals (JSTOR, 1996b).
JSTOR became available officially in January, 1997. The project's goal is to provide the complete runs for at least 100 critical journal titles in a ten to fifteen year timespan (JSTOR, 1996c). The archive stores both images and text. Images are used to deliver information to users; text is used to search the archives. JSTOR functions as an archive, and does not publish journals. Additionally, JSTOR has begun to work with electronic journal publishers to provide access to back issues through the JSTOR archives. To access JSTOR, users need an Internet connection, a 17-inch monitor, an Internet browser (JSTOR has a preference for Netscape), and a post-script printer.

Negotiations with publishers continue, and publishers from political science, population and demography, and mathematics have signed licensing agreements with JSTOR. Clusters of journals in major fields of study are being compiled to permit scholars to search across titles in related disciplines. Consult the World Wide Web for further information on JSTOR at http://www.jstor.org/about/index.html.

OCLC Electronic Journals Online OCLC's Electronic Journals Online, or EJO, is an online service that provides access to 48 journals available via the Internet or through dial access. The full-text of each journal is provided, including figures, tables, and equations. Access to EJO is provided through PC-based Guidon software which was developed by OCLC for use with Microsoft Windows.
EJO provides

- an integrated approach to information dissemination;
- reduces the need for hardware systems and training;
- provides new ways to use the serials collection;
- reduces serial costs through elimination of binding and replacement costs;
- and provides costs savings in subscriptions (OCLC, 1996b).

The titles can be integrated into the existing workflow used for print journals. Possible benefits of EJO for publishers include:

- speeding up the publication process for journals;
- allowing for the publication of lengthy studies and full data;
- making journals interactive through use of e-mail letters to the editor, etc.;
- reducing the impact of decreasing print subscriptions;
- reducing distribution costs since there are no ongoing printing or mailing costs.

(OCLC, 1996b)

Some of the benefits of EJO for users are:

- providing full-text to users on demand;
- allowing superior navigation;
- providing all information included on the printed page;
- the ability to connect to related resources through hypertext links to related external bibliographic databases, references, and articles available in other OCLC electronic journals

(OCLC, 1996b).

Information on EJO is available on the World Wide Web at http://medusa.prod.oclc.org:3050/html/ejo__homepage.htm.

Oxford University Press (OUP) OUP publishes over 160 scholarly journals, and each title has its own Web page (links are provided through OUP's home page). The home pages provide abstracts from current and back issues, information on editorial boards, subscription information, and sample electronic issues for some titles. In addition, some titles provide electronic delivery of full-text articles and graphics two weeks before the print version is available. Some titles are multimedia journals (*Neurocase, Medical Image Analysis, Human Reproduction Update*). OUP also offers Journals Awareness Service, which provides a searchable, regularly updated database of information for all titles. The OUP Home Page provides links to sample issues, examples of multimedia journals, and the Journals Awareness Service, and is available at http://www.oup.co.uk/jnls/.

Project Muse Project Muse makes scholarly electronic journals published by Johns Hopkins University Press available to libraries. As of May 1996, fifteen titles were available online; an additional 28 titles are under consideration for inclusion by December 1996 (Johns Hopkins University Press, 1996b). Project Muse is available by subscription and permits unrestricted printing on demand. Each journal has its own individual URL, and provides the complete text, including advertisement and classifieds. The service provides hypertext links, Boolean searching capability, and the ability to create hot lists of frequently used titles. Users may search by full-text, article, author, or keyword in a single journal, in specific journals, or in all journals. Information on Project Muse is available on the World Wide Web at http://calliope.jhu.edu.

Red Sage Project The University of California, San Francisco, AT&T Bell Laboratories, and Springer-Verlag collaborated to produce the Red Sage Electronic Journal Project. The project began on January 1, 1993, and officially concluded on December 31, 1996. Access to some titles from the project continued until April 1, 1997. All publishers involved with the project declined to continue the experiment (University of California, San Francisco and Center for Knowledge Management,

1997). This is not surprising since the Web now provides a variety of ways for publishers to provide electronic journals to end users. The intent of the Project was to provide faculty, students, and staff with online access to an electronic library of biomedical and clinical journals such as the *New England Journal of Medicine* and the *Journal of the American Medical Association* (Red Sage Project, 1996). The purpose of the project was to test the electronic distribution of journals directly to individuals' desktops. Users were able to browse online journals page by page, select current or back issues, and print articles. AT&T Bell Laboratories RightPages software was used to include the full-text of each journal on the screen to provide the look and feel of a print journal (Red Sage Project, 1996). Titles in the Project were arranged alphabetically, with the most current issues on top. Clicking on journal icons or tables of contents allowed users to retrieve the articles they wanted. It is interesting to note that journals used for the Project were organized in a manner similar to that used in most libraries and combined with RightPages software to make the journals easy to use and presented them in a familiar, easy to read format. Information on the Red Sage Project is available on the World Wide Web at http://www.library.ucsf.edu/lib/gen/redsage.html. An overview of the RightPages system is available at http://www.ckm.ucsf.edu/Projects/RedSage/Overview.html.

SuperJournal SuperJournal is a project which is part of the British Electronic Libraries Programme (eLib). It is a collaboration of publishers, universities, and libraries to develop multimedia electronic journals. SuperJournal began in December 1995, and has funding for three years. The journals are mounted on a host server and delivered via JANET and SuperJANET networks to end users at library test sites. The journals are peer reviewed publications which have established reputations as print publications. The first journals were delivered to test sites in December 1996. The project's goals are:

- to determine the features and functionality that make electronic journals useful to readers;
- to determine the benefits from the author's point of view of publishing in an electronic journal and what conditions are needed to encourage them to do so;
- to understand what is required from publishers to develop electronic journals;
- to understand what is required for local institutions and their libraries to provide electronic journals to readers.

(SuperJournal Project, 1997).

The SuperJournal Home Page is located at http://www.superjournal.ac.uk/sj/project.htm.

The University Licensing Project (TULIP) and Elsevier Electronic Subscriptions (EES) TULIP is a collaboration that began between Elsevier Science and ten American universities in 1991 and concluded in 1996. The project's goal was to jointly test systems for networked delivery to, and use of journals at, the user's desktop. The Optical Character Recognition (OCR) generated 'raw' ASCII full-text of 43 Elsevier and Pergamon materials science and engineering journals, were provided by Elsevier Science to the universities which developed or adapted systems to deliver these journals to the desktops of their end users (Elsevier Science, 1996).

Participants set the following goals:

* to determine the feasibility of networked distribution to institutions with different levels of sophistication in their technical infrastructures;
* to examine alternative costing, pricing, subscription and market models that may be used successfully in electronic distribution;
* to compare electronic prototypes with existing print distribution models;
* to study reader usage patterns according to different types of journal distribution.

(Elsevier Science, 1996)

The project revealed that the attraction of full-text/image products is convenience.

The TULIP project allowed Elsevier to make better decisions on how to proceed with the conversion from print to electronic, how to store and distribute electronic materials, and what type of customer support is necessary when providing electronic information. Elsevier Science concluded from the project that managing large digital collections locally is harder and more expensive than handling comparable print collections. It was apparent that not all libraries are ready to handle digital collections and will not be prepared in the near future (Elsevier Science, 1996). Elsevier Science also believes that users will only move to using electronic journals when they find the content they need in sufficient quantity. The project revealed that print publishing requires little local training or support, while electronic publishing is more complicated and requires a different type of involvement from the publisher (Elsevier Science, 1996). The TULIP Final Report is available on the World Wide Web at http://www.elsevier.nl:80/homepage/about/resproj/trmenu.htm.

Following the TULIP project is the Elsevier Electronic Subscriptions program (EES) which was launched in 1995 to provide electronic versions of Elsevier's research and professional print titles and offers libraries complete electronic editions in addition to or in place of print titles (Elsevier Science, 1995). The service provides access to about 1200

Elsevier Science journals published under the imprints of Elsevier, Pergamon, North-Holland, and Butterworth-Heinemann. EES provides full-length scientific articles, all editorial material, including product reviews, correspondence, editorial notes, etc. This service offers added functionality such as simultaneous access and desktop access, and is intended to increase the access and volume of information available to users (Elsevier Science, 1995). Unlike TULIP, EES is delivered on magnetic tape or CD-ROM, and is updated weekly or bi-weekly, depending on the customer. EES files are implemented using a library's existing software or third party software. Additionally, Elsevier has been working with OCLC to provide access to EES titles using OCLC's SiteSearch system, which is used to create and maintain local databases. Information on EES is available on the World Wide Web at http://www-east.elsevier.com/ees/qa.htm.

Contents Direct is a direct alerting service for Elsevier Science's journals. This service delivers contents pages by e-mail via a service similiar to listserv. Contents Direct provides information on editorial board appointments, calls for papers, announcement of special issues and discounts on new books, for example. At this time, only Elsevier Science journals are provided through Contents Direct, but there are plans to include more journals in the future. Subscribers may submit a request to have a favorite journal title added to the service by sending an e-mail to j.silver@ elsevier.co.uk. Additional information on Contents Direct is available on http://www. elsevier.nl/inca/homepage/about/caware/condir/.

Document Delivery Services

This discussion will focus on document delivery services that receive or transmit information electronically, and does not include all standard companies. Will document delivery services be the wave of the future as the price of print journals continues to rise and commercial vendors begin to provide access to electronic journals? Formerly, libraries held a monopoly on document delivery due to collections and fair use rights. Some libraries still continue to compete with commercial providers. Libraries may begin to outsource serials related functions while concentrating on providing other core services such as reference, bibliographic instruction, and cataloging. It is possible that libraries will permit vendors to handle serials functions since they will no longer be able to cover subscription and binding costs as storage space decreases, and there is little time to archive or provide service to back issues. It is likely that libraries will begin to provide access to serials through citation and document delivery services, through database vendors such as DIALOG, on CD-ROM products such as ABI/Inform, through consortia such as the Committee on Institutional Cooperation, or through electronic delivery from companies such as Elsevier and OCLC. While serials will continue to have a central role in the provision of timely information, libraries may invest less time and effort maintaining on-site collections.

Document delivery services provide options for the request and delivery of materials. Many services are available to both individuals and libraries. Document delivery services aim to provide convenience through electronic transmission of information. Convenience often comes at a cost, however. Some article and citation delivery services charge a fee for the article, plus copyright costs, and an article can cost as much as $12. The tradeoff is quick access to the desired information. Document delivery services also offer an attractive option to traditional interlibrary loan. Eiblum (1995) notes: 'Since 1991 notable changes have occurred in every aspect of document delivery. Identifying, locating and procuring copies of articles is no longer a hit-or-miss exercise involving manual reference sources.' Document delivery services have become one of the central services offered by many libraries. Some of the advantages provided by document delivery services include:

- articles from different publishers will be offered by one service and do not require a subscription or arrangement with each publisher;
- users pay only for articles received;
- it is useful for accessing articles and titles with low use that do not warrant a subscription.

(Machovec, 1997).

In early 1997, Wayne Perrin (1997) of Macmillan Publishers UK, circulated a survey on the future impact of electronic delivery of information on the print publishing industry, particularly publishers of humanities and social sciences monographs. The survey was distributed to a number of listservs. There was a general agreement from respondents that there is a demand by faculty members for desktop delivery of information. The primary reason cited for moving to electronic document delivery was to provide improved access, particularly for students. The majority of respondents believe they will be providing desktop delivery of information within the next five years. Interestingly, more respondents indicated that electronic document delivery would be the most important medium for students since they are often better prepared to accept this service than older faculty members.

Some of the leading vendors and suppliers are mentioned below.

ADONIS ADONIS provides a CD-ROM document delivery service (Document Delivery (DD)) that includes about 740 journals, predominantly biomedical, representing the most highly cited titles in their respective fields (ADONIS, 1996c). Seventy-five publishers participate in the service, including Academic Press, Blackwell, Chapman and Hall,

Elsevier Science, Kluwer Academic Publishers, and Pergamon Press. The service provides high-quality PDF and tagged image format (TIFF) images of scientific journal articles. The articles can be viewed on screen or printed on demand. Subscribers receive one or two CD-ROMs per week containing more than 90 journal issues each. Journals included in ADONIS arc not scanned cover-to-cover but do include all articles, letters to editors, valedictories, and obituaries. ADONIS prides itself on its conversion record. It takes two and a half weeks, or twelve working days, from receipt of a print journal issue to its storage (with a full bibliographic index) on CD-ROM to delivery to libraries.

The advantages of using ADONIS include reduced shelf space, a secure way to archive journals, and expansion of a library's holdings while reducing reliance on interlibrary loan (ADONIS, 1996e). More information on this service is available at http://www.adonis.nl/ddesdd.htm.

British Library Document Supply Centre (BLDSC) The BLDSC provides a document delivery services to libraries and individuals worldwide. Requests may be sent via ARTTel (Automated Request Transmission by Telecommunications) which is used for electronic requests or via e-mail through ARTEmail (British Library Document Supply Centre, 1996b) . Requests through ARTEmail require a system with access to the Internet or JANET. Documents may also be requested by mail or fax. Requests are normally handled within 24–48 hours of receipt, and copies are sent by first-class mail. New developments include OPAC97, which became available in May 1997, and provides free access via the Web to seven catalogs that cover the major collections of the British Library in London and Boston Spa. Users can search the holdings and order items through a user interface. Information on the British Library Document Supply Centre is available on the World Wide Web at http://portico.bl.uk/dsc/.

CitaDel CitaDel is a citation and document delivery service provided by the Research Libraries Group (RLG) which provides information taken from general and specific interest databases which include journals, newspapers, conference proceedings, dissertations, and other publications at the individual article level. Two search interfaces are provided by CitaDel:

- Eureka, a search service designed for end users on campuses and in libraries;
- Zephyr, a Z39.50 service which allows institutions to use the commands and formats of their online systems to provide access to RLG's data.

(Research Libraries Group, 1996c)

Current CitaDel files include the *Avery Index to Architectural Periodicals, Ei Page One, History of Science and Technology,* and *Public Affairs Information Service (PAI).* CitaDel offers online document ordering for *ABI/INFORM, Global Edition* from UMI (articles from business magazines, management and professional publications, academic journals, trade and specialty publications, and international titles), *Ei Page One* from UMI (papers and articles from over 5400 national and international conference proceedings and engineering journals), *Inside Information PLUS* from the BLDSC (a current-awareness database which provides author, title, and journal citation information for articles appearing in 21000 of the most frequently requested titles in the BLDSC's collection), *Newspaper Abstracts* from UMI (a source for articles from 27 major national, regional, and financial newspapers), and *Periodical Abstracts, Research II Edition* from UMI (an index to popular and academic journals).

Documents may be delivered by postal mail, fax, or Ariel, RLG's document transmission service. RLG describes Ariel as faster, more reliable, and less expensive than fax, and produces images of greater resolution and quality (Research Libraries Group, 1996b). Turnaround time is from within two days of receipt of request (fax and Ariel) to six to ten days for postal mail. Information on CitaDel is available on the World Wide Web at http://www.rlg.org/citadel.html.

Delft University of Technology Library Documents may be requested from Delft University Library (DUTL) in a number of ways. About 90% of articles requested from DUTLcan be supplied immediately from its own holdings. If DUTL is unable to fill a request, it is sent automatically to other libraries within the Netherlands. Requests can be placed by mail, telephone, fax, using an online Web request form, or directly through the LIS. Rush processing of requests is available and take about 25 hours to process. Rush requests can be made by mail, telephone, or fax. Further information on DUTL document deliver is available at http://www.library.tudelft.nl.BTUD/eng/rqinfoe.htm.

FIDDO FIDDO is a project funded by the Joint Information Systems Committee's (JISC) Electronic Libraries Programme, under the supporting Studies Programme. The project's goal is to provide library and information managers with information that permits them to make decisions about the feasibility, selection, and implementation of electronic document delivery systems for their institutions (FIDDO Project, 1996). Two projects funded by eLib are EDDIS and the InfoBike. EDDIS, or Electronic Document Delivery Integrated Solution, is a project which aims to produce an integrated document delivery system driven by end users which will include holdings and an article document delivery systems. InfoBike's mission is to provide end users with the ability to conduct database searches, electronically request items, and get full-text items delivered to their desktops. Partners in this project are Bath University, Academic Press, Blackwell Science, the Consortium of Academic Libraries in Manchester, ICL, Keele University, Kent University, and Staffordshire University.

Institute de l'Information Scientifique et Technique (INIST) INIST is a service unit of the Centre National de la Recherche Science (CNRS) and operates under the supervision of the French Ministry of Higher Education and Research. INIST's collections include major world scientific and technical literature. It uses a computerized order management system to quickly process requests for copies of documents. There are 23 000 titles with 9200 current subscriptions in the INIST periodical collection. INIST also has a report collection which includes 56 000 scientific reports from public and private research organizations. There is also a proceedings collection that contains 60 000 proceedings from major international conferences and learned society meetings. Lastly, INIST provides French doctoral dissertations from 1985 on (about 100 000 dissertations).

INIST participates in several European library projects and is involved in standardization activities involving electronic document structuring and protocol definition for electronic document exchange in document management systems. For more information, consult the INIST Web page at http://www.inist.fr/anglais/fdpang/fondsang.htm.

KR SourceOne KR SourceOne is a service provided by Knight-Ridder Information, Inc. that delivers information from a worldwide collection of libraries with more than 1.5 million titles (Knight-Ridder Information, Inc., 1996). The information collection includes digitally stored documents available in full-text including all original columns, figures, graphs, tables, and drawings. Digitally stored documents include the UMI ABI/Inform Article Collection, the U.S. Patents Collection, and European Patent Applications. Requests can be made by phone, fax, or e-mail, or ordered online through DIALOG and DataStar databases. Delivery is provided through mail, express mail, courier, fax, e-mail, or FTP. Documents can be faxed within two hours or hardcopy may be sent in one business day. Documents from the patent collection may be sent by e-mail. A form is also available for Web-based ordering. Information on KR SourceOne is available on the World Wide Web at http://www.krinfo.com/krsourceone/.

UMI UMI offers two services, InfoStore and ProQuest. The InfoStore is a full-service document supplier which can provide journal articles, dissertations, technical reports, conference proceedings, etc. Documents may be sent by fax, courier, or mail. All documents received from the

InfoStore are copyright cleared. An online form is provided for ordering via the Web. Information on the InfoStore is available on the World Wide Web at http://www.umi.com/infostore.

ProQuest is a service that offers full-text, full-image, or can combine searchable text with graphs, charts, maps, and photographs (UMI, 1996a). This service provides abstracts and indexes for over 3,000 titles, and all articles are copyright cleared. Documents are delivered by fax, express delivery, or postal mail. ProQuest is available through the Web, and in Z39.50 and Windows environments. Documents may be delivered to a user's desktop or may be ordered through the UMI InfoStore. Information on ProQuest is available on the World Wide Web at http://pqdbeta.umi.com/ad/pdirect/.

UnCover   UnCover is an online periodical article delivery service which indexes almost 17,000 English language periodicals. There are over 7 million articles available through online ordering, and articles appear in UnCover at the same time that they are included in the current periodical issues from which they are taken (UnCover Company, 1996). Access is provided to some of the major university and public libraries in the US, and also to some European and Australian libraries. Requests may be made by fax, phone, or e-mail. By telnetting to database.carl.org., users may also access UnCover. Additionally, UnCover is also available through Blackwell's CONNECT Service. Articles are sent by fax, often within 24 hours. Information on UnCover is available on the World Wide Web at http://www.carl.org/uncover/what.html.

Implications of document delivery services for libraries

Document delivery services have implications for the role of libraries in the provision of information. Many document delivery services cater directly to individuals, eliminating libraries from the process. Information that is normally provided to users free or for nominal fees by libraries will be sold to them by commercial vendors. This trend, combined with the increasing number of commercial publishers which offer electronic serials packages, may lead to the commercialization and privatization of information which is at the core of reference service. Libraries may use these services to augment their collections and services as they continue to cancel journal subscriptions and cut back on services. Document delivery services may also benefit libraries by providing an additional avenue of information for interlibrary loan.

The number and type of document delivery services indicates that it is likely that they will continue to grow in popularity. Many of these services are advertised on the Web, and appeal to the increasing number of users who rely on electronic information. Using these services can eliminate the need to visit the library altogether. Libraries will have to reevaluate the level of commitment that will be devoted to providing this type of information, or possibly relinquish this role to commercial vendors. The growing popularity of the Web, combined with a number of powerful search engines, have provided many end users with the opportunity to be more self-reliant in the information seeking process. The increase in document delivery services is also part of the continuing trend towards end-user access.

Chapter 4

Interactive Multimedia, Virtual Libraries, and Digital Libraries

Interactive Multimedia

This chapter will discuss applications of interactive multimedia in libraries, plus some newer technological developments: specifically, virtual and digital libraries. As libraries move into the electronic age, virtual and digital libraries will become more prevalent. Although it is doubtful that any library will close its doors and offer only electronic access to services and resources, it is becoming increasingly common for libraries to provide information and to collaborate electronically.

Interactive multimedia initially were heralded as one of the most dynamic new technologies to emerge in years. However, the widespread implementation and use of this technology that was originally anticipated has not taken place. While CD-ROMs are commonly believed to embody interactive multimedia since the technology is frequently available in this format, interactive multimedia are by no means limited to CD-ROMs. They may also be found on the Internet or in other formats, such as videorecordings. Jizba *et al.* (1994, p. 1) define interactive multimedia as ' . . .media residing in one or more physical carriers (videodiscs, computer disks, computer optical discs, computer audio discs, etc.) or on computer networks.' Interactive multimedia are user-controlled, and employ nonlinear navigation using computer technology. One of the distinguishing features of interactive multimedia is that no two users will have the same experience using them. Unlike computer programs or games, there is no preset path of navigation. The outcome is completely controlled by the user's actions.

Interactive multimedia integrate multiple media and sources to communicate information at many levels of abstraction, such as digitized tones and speech, bitmapped graphics, text, and live and recorded video (Grinstein and Ward, 1996). 'Other genres are based to a large degree on the type of information they convey, regardless of the form of presentation or access mechanism' (Demas, 1994, p.73). Interactive multimedia differ from other presentation formats in that they are entirely based on the form of presentation, rather than type(s) of information provided.

Interactive multimedia allow users to explore information in whatever order suits their needs. They can easily be tailored to the needs and learning styles of a variety of users, and for this reason are well suited to educational programs and library applications. Interactive technology enhance the way in which people learn since more than text-based access is provided. Total access to information is provided because users rely on more than one sense to access the materials. Other applications of interactive multimedia include authoring and production tools, and graphics and visualization (Grinstein and Ward, 1996).

Digital libraries, interactive television, training, education, presentations, and simulations use interactive multimedia in a variety of ways. More recent implementations of interactive multimedia have been made available on the World Wide Web. A program called Shockwave for Directors recently made possible interactive graphics, sound, and animation on the Internet. Shockwave requires a plug-in, which is a file containing data that may alter, enhance, or extend functions provided by a parent application, while an application is a 'complete, self-contained program that performs a specific function directly for the user' (Howe, 1996). To sample the Shockwave plug-in, visit the Macromedia home page on the World Wide Web at http://www.macromedia.com/shockwave/.

Other typical library applications of interactive multimedia include tutorials and interactive encyclopedias and reference tools. A discussion of various applications and products follows.

LibraryTutor LibraryTutor is an interactive program originally designed and used by Wascana Institute of Regina, Saskatchewan, Canada to train students how to use the library. It is designed to allow users to learn at their own pace. Ten modules are featured:

- computer basics;
- guided tour a tour of a generic library is provided, covering those areas found in most libraries;
- arrangement of materials – the major classification schemes (Library of Congress, Dewey Decimal Classification, Superintendent of Documents Classification) are explained;
- finding information – catalogs, indexes and abstracts are discussed;
- types of materials – books, reference materials, serials, special collections, and subject files are covered;
- electronic resources – electronic delivery systems, searching, types of databases and the Internet are discussed;

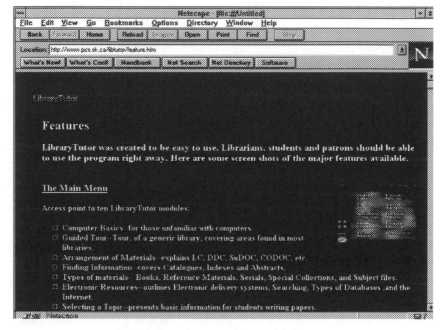

Figure 4.1 LibraryTutor Features page.
Source: *pcsinc@sasknet.sk.ca*

- selecting a topic – basic information for students writing papers is included;
- conducting a search – search steps, strategies, hints, and problems are covered;
- evaluating information – evaluative criteria are discussed;
- documentation – footnotes, end notes, bibliographies, and examples from style guides are provided.

Most pages include illustrations, and users can easily move between pages. Some sections also include video clips, and narration is provided or may be turned off at the user's preference. A glossary, keyword index, and help screens are also included. Bookmarks may be used to mark sections for future use. Additional information and a preview of LibraryTutor are available on the World Wide Web at http:// www.pcs.sk.ca/libtutor/ (See Figure 4.1.).

Grolier Interactive offers a number of reference tools that are widely used by libraries. These products represent one of the more common applications of interactive multimedia, and examples include the *1997 Grolier Multimedia Encyclopedia*, the *1996 Guiness Multimedia Disc* *of Records*, and the *Multimedia Encyclopedia of Science Fiction*. The *Multimedia Encyclopedia* includes a world atlas with more than 1200 maps plus links to related articles. It provides interactive features such as animation, movies, and cut-away illustrations. Four interface themes are available which permit users to customize searches. *The Guiness Multimedia Disc of Records*, in addition to providing the superlative and random records found in the print version, provides video clips which allows users to watch a sky diver or see a Concorde fly, for example. The *Multimedia Encyclopedia of Science Fiction* includes video and audio interviews, film stills and trailers, and hyperlinks and cross-references. Further information on Grolier Interactive reference products may be located at http://gi.grolier.com/gi.html.

Yahoo! employs interactive multimedia in its Recreation section (Recreation: Games: Internet Games: Interactive Games: Interactive Fiction). The section on interactive fiction includes 'add-to stories.' In *S.P.Q.R.: The Virtual Rome* (http://pathfinder.com/@@8Ez5GAQA372 zjX39/twep/rome/), for example, users must register and participate as Roman citizens in the 4th century. Tools are provided for users to create their own interactive adventure stories. A section on add-to stories features a number of scenarios in which users contribute to stories which are intended to be continued indefinitely. In each case, the user is an active participant in the process, and no two users will have the same experience. Visit Yahoo's interactive fiction site on the World Wide Web at http://www.yahoo.com/Recreation/Games/Interactive—Fiction/ (See Figure 4.2).

The Place is an experimental Web art site created and maintained by Joseph Squier, who describes it as 'an evolving repository of artwork created specifically for distribution the Web' (Squier, 1996). The emphasis of the Place is on graphics and images, and it contains stories, photographs, images, and poems. Users can navigate through the stories and images in a random, self-directed fashion. The artwork is constantly changed and updated, and may be visited on the World Wide Web at http://gertrude.art.uiuc.edu/ludgate/the/place/place2.html (See Figures 4.3–4.5.)

Virtual libraries

The characteristics that make interactive multimedia attractive for teaching purposes and reference tools are also what help to make them accessible and easy to use by a variety of users. Virtual libraries rely on interactivity to allow patrons to explore sites and to use resources. While the terms 'virtual library' and 'digital library' are frequently used

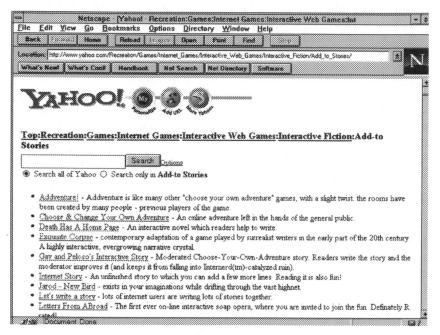

Figure 4.2 Yahoo! Top:Recreation:Games:Internet Games:Interactive Web Games:Interactive Fiction main page.
Source: *online form*
Text and artwork copywrite 1996 by Yahoo!, INC. YAHOO! and the YAHOO!
logo are trademarks of YAHOO! INC.

interchangeably, they are in fact not the same thing. A digital library consists of a networked collection of multimedia information typically available in one location, while a virtual library comprises a set of links to various resources on the Internet, such as documents, software or databases. The links in a virtual library are transparent to users, and it provides them with one interface to information. Covi and Kling (1996) found through their research that computer scientists and library and information scientists define digital libraries a little differently. Computer scientists define digital libraries as collections of full-text documents and images available through Internet services like ftp, gopher, and the Web. In contrast, library and information scientists view digital libraries as including automated card catalogs, search citation collections, abstracting services, and services such as DIALOG that provide full-text. The advantage of a virtual library is that it can transparently provide access to collections that are not geographically close to each other. A virtual library is not designed to reside in one place

Figure 4.3 The Place main page.
Source: *joseph@pobox.com (permission granted)*

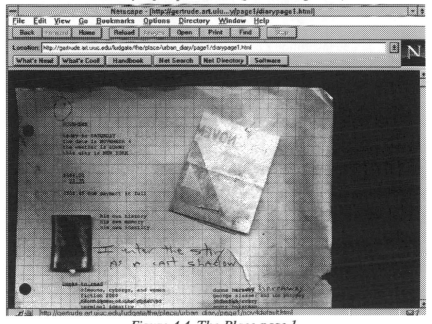

Figure 4.4 The Place page 1.
Source: *joseph@pobox.com (permission granted)*

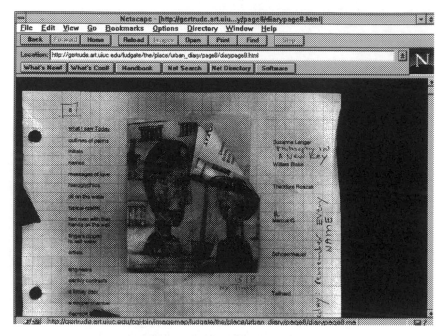

Figure 4.5   The Place page 8.
Source: *joseph@pobox.com (permission granted)*

(such as on one institution's computer system) in the manner of a digital library. A number of Web sites bill themselves as virtual libraries, as do some LISs. This may not be completely inaccurate.

Virtual libraries encourage collaborative efforts and information sharing between institutions, particularly those separated by a great distance. The concept of the virtual library draws on one of the themes central to the mission of libraries: access. Furthermore, virtual libraries ensure that no one is denied access to a collection. Virtual libraries serve an educational role in that they provide access to collections and services that are often not available to the general public. They help to publicize an institution's resources and services, and like interactive multimedia, permit users to proceed at their own pace. Interestingly, in his 1994 article 'The virtual library: what is it and where are we headed?' Harden states that some individuals believe the virtual library will make librarians obsolete, while others believe it will increase their professional stature.

Ames Public Library, Ames, Iowa The Ames Public Library's Web page offers a virtual tour of the library, complete with photographs and detailed information. The virtual tour (including directions) visits the information desk, youth services, media services, circulation services, the bookmobile, and includes a look at two behind the scenes departments: technical services and administration. Users can choose where they want to visit, and links are provided for forward and backward movement. For more information on the virtual tour or the library, visit the library's Web site at http://mirage.scl.ameslab.gov/jc/library/vt.html (See Figures 4.6 and 4.7).

Global Campus Project The California State University campuses at Long Beach, San Jose, Chico, and Cal Poly San Luis Obispo have collaborated with each other institutions to build an electronic 'Global Campus' which will be fully accessible to anyone using the Internet. The Global Campus contains a variety of educational materials, such as images, sounds, text, and video to be used for nonprofit, educational purposes. 'The goals of the project are to share resources through technology, to provide a means for institutions to make their resources available to others worldwide while respecting intellectual property, and to provide high quality materials for instructional development' (Global Campus, 1996). The Global Campus provides resources on business, engineering, fine and liberal arts, and science. Links are also provided to other projects. Information on the Global Campus may be found on the World Wide Web at http://www.csulb.edu/gc.

The Internet Public Library The Internet Public Library (IPL) is one of the better known virtual libraries on the World Wide Web. The IPL defines itself as 'the first public library of and for the Internet community; an experiment, trying to discover and promote the most effective roles and contributions of librarians to the Internet and vice versa' (Internet Public Library, 1996b). The IPL's mission is to find, evaluate, select, organize, and create information resources.

The IPL began as a graduate seminar at the School of Information at the University of Michigan in 1995. The seminar's goal was to explore the relationship of libraries, librarians, and librarianship within a distributed networked environment. Work began January 5, 1995, and the IPL opened for business on March 17, 1995 (Internet Public Library, 1996b). The IPL is now a grant-funded operation with a full-time staff. The site's content is constantly changing and being updated. The IPL welcomes visitors at its Web site at http://www.ipl.org.

THOR+ THOR+ is the virtual library of the Libraries of Purdue University. It provides access to a virtual reference desk as well as to subject reading rooms, electronic journals, and libraries around the globe. The virtual reference desk is similar to that found on the Web pages of many libraries, and provides access to government documents, information

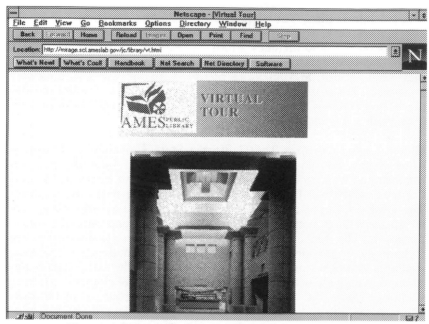

Figure 4.6 Ames Public Library virtual tours page.
Source: *gmillsap@ames.lib.ia.us*

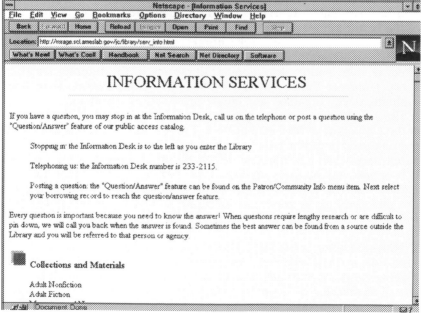

Figure 4.7 Ames Public Library text-based information page.
Source: *gmillsap@ames.lib.ia.us*

technology, dictionaries, phone books, maps, zip code information, and other reference sources. The subject reading rooms are divided into five areas: humanities, social sciences, natural sciences, physical science and mathematics, and engineering and technology. The Virtual Library may be accessed through the Libraries of Purdue University Web page at http://thorplus.lib.purdue.edu/vlibrary/. (See Figures 4.8–4.9).

VIVA VIVA is a consortium of the libraries of 39 state supported colleges and universities in Virginia, including George Mason University, community colleges, Norfolk State University, and Old Dominion. VIVA's mission is to provide enhanced access to library and information resources for the Commonwealth of Virginia's academic libraries (VIVA, 1996). The collection includes:

- books and other electronic texts, including University of Virginia's electronic text library and Virginia Tech's Scholarly Communications Project;
- image databases, including Virginia Tech's Digital Image Collection and the University of Virginia's Virginia Online Atlas;
- journals, indexes with full-text articles and Library of Congress' newspaper and current periodicals room;
- news sources such as CNN interactive, the *New York Times*, and *USA Today*;
- reference works and indexes, including *ABI/Inform*, *AGRICOLA*, and the *Oxford English Dictionary*;
- special collections, including digitized collections from the Library of Virginia, Virginia Military Institute, and the Mariners' Museum.

Visit the VIVA home page at http://www.viva.lib.va.us.

Digital Libraries

A current focus for many libraries is to digitize information and make it available online. Hawkins (1994, p. 27) feels that the concept of the digital library violates some traditional assumptions about libraries and collections. He believes that there should be a move away from the concept of the library as a physical place, and that libraries and collections are about much more than books. The concept of the digital library defines it as a repository of all kinds of information which is not subject to limitations of format or physical space.

The co-existence of print and digital documents presents problems for libraries. Decisions should be made regarding which resources should be converted to digital format, and guidelines are needed to reach these decisions. The types of information that are digitized range from course reserves to rare documents. Covi and Kling (1996) discovered through

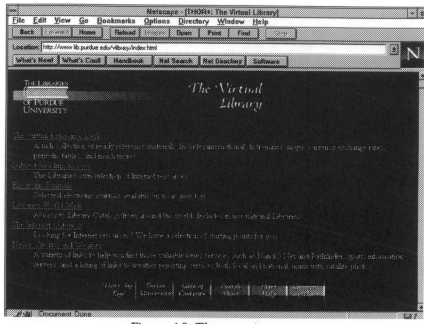

Figure 4.8 Thor+ main page.
Source: *webmaster@thorplus.lib.purdue.ed*

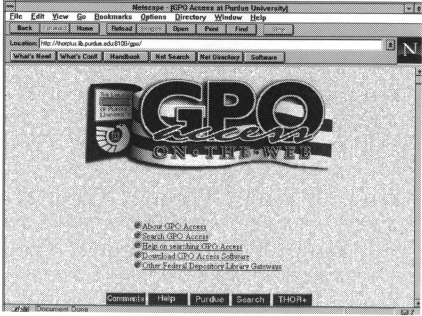

Figure 4.9 Thor+ reference page.
Source: *webmaster@thorplus.lib.-purdue.ed*

their study that academic administrators often based decisions regarding digital materials on local indications of demand, such as the number of people who use the Web for their work, demand for e-mail accounts, and the number of requests to use bibliographic databases. This leads to the question of whether digital libraries should be tailored to individual groups or communities. Some library professionals believe that digital documents encourage users to take a more active role in learning since they may directly seek out the information needed rather than having to access a broad set of information that may be potentially useful.

Hawkins (1994, p. 24) describes the digital library concept as 'specifically both a solution to the economic problems facing libraries and a vehicle for a new functionality that promises to transform scholarship and bring the cultural, social, and economic benefits of information to the many.' Traditionally, libraries owned the information provided for their users, and the amount of information which a library owned was an indication of its quality and standing. With digital libraries, the ability to provide effective access to information has become the measure of a library's quality.

Collection development is still a concern for digital libraries. Graham (1995, p. 332) further asserts that with experience, libraries will realize that there is still a responsibility for collection development and management with digital libraries. He states:

> It is sometimes loosely proposed (not by librarians) that libraries need not acquire electronic information, for it will be available somewhere on the network. Such proposals ignore the obvious truth that some institution must still, in the end, take responsibility for the information.
>
> (1995, p. 332)

Duplication between digital collections is unlikely since existence in one location generally permits worldwide access. With digital libraries, there will not be extensive duplication of resources as it now exists. Some degree of duplication is necessary for sociological and economic reasons, for example, because since access to one site may not be available at a given time, or because sites close or relocate. Electronic information is vulnerable, and the value of a collection is based on coherence rather than individual items. Private collections do not last indefinitely since materials are lost, stolen, or damaged. Mirror sites are an option that provides security for digital collections. This type of site is used to store copies of some, or all, the files from another site, and makes than more easily (and quickly) available to local users. It also reduces the load on any particular site by making a number of sites available. Mirror sites are often located in a number of countries world wide. For example, the original site may be in London and there may be mirror sites in France, Turkey and the United States. Digital libraries ensure stability, and libraries must guarantee that information will be available and is useful.

Butler (1996, p. 127) describes the difference between digital library applications and traditional library automation as the ability to manage intellectual property rights dynamically at the document or subdocument level according to license agreements or permission conditions. Some advantages which digital libraries provide over their print counterparts include:

- guaranteed availability of information – information is always accessible and not limited by physical location, number of copies, or circulation status;
- facilities and benefits are offered which are not possible in a traditional library environment – user profiles may be maintained to provide a mechanism to inform users of recent technological developments;
- elimination of traditional collection management operations – functions such as binding, preservation, and shelving are no longer required.

(Catenazzi and Sommaruga, 1995, p. 128).

Cost is also a concern for digital libraries. Chapman and Kenney (1996) question the cost effectiveness of digital libraries, and feel they will be most cost effective if the following assumptions are true:

- libraries can share digital collections;
- digital collections will alleviate the need to support full traditional libraries at the local level;
- electronic access will increase use;
- the long-term value of digital collections will exceed the costs associated with their maintenance and delivery.

A digital library may involve organizing a library's electronic documents into an organized collection, or converting a print library into an electronic library. There are five interface designs for digital libraries (Catenazi and Sommaruga, 1995, pp. 129–131):

1. plain text interface. This is the simplest and most immediate method of presenting information. ASCII text is used, and no images or multimedia images are included. The advantage of this approach is that it permits universal accessibility of documents. No special equipment or retrieval techniques are needed. The drawback is that a poor interface is provided, and the text is commonly displayed through scrolling windows. This type of display is unattractive, frequently difficult to read, and cumbersome to navigate.

2. image-based interface. Most information in digital collections is presented as images, and only some portions, such as a table of contents, may be converted to text. This process is typically used when documents are converted from an existing print collection. The benefit of this approach is that it preserves the integrity of the original document. The disadvantage of this interface is that it requires an enormous amount of storage space.

3. hypertext-based interface. Documents using this interface are presented and organized using hypertext links. This method provides a powerful mechanism for organizing and accessing information, but may also be confusing to users.

4. book-like interface. With this interface, documents are presented in a book format. This approach is popular with users since information is structured in a manner that is quite familiar and easy for them to use.

5. mixed strategy. This approach employs a combination of two or more of the previously mentioned interfaces.

Audience and intended purpose of the collection should first be carefully considered when designing digital libraries. Features that should be considered in planning are:

- browsing;
- searching;
- ability to customize;
- printing capability.

Browsing should provide navigation choices, including hierarchical navigation (links from the table of contents), linear navigation (forward and backwards movement through the document), transversely (links across the document and across the digital collection), and direct access (provides access to specific locations, such as table of contents, list of figures or tables, etc.) (Catenazzi and Sommaruga, 1995, pp. 131–132).

Hawkins (1994, p. 25) believes one of the benefits of digital collections is that they will create a new dimension of scholarship and education. Digital collections can help to remove the divisions between the information rich and poor by providing universal access to information. With digital libraries, borrowing privileges, physical location, etc. are not what matters. The important issue is whether or not a user can access the information needed. Digital libraries may also raise the question of what types of information literacy skills are required to use the collection. Libraries need to determine who will need to be taught and how. It is not safe to assume that a digital library is necessarily self-explanatory.

One of the advantages of digital collections is that users can search large amounts of information quickly. The disadvantages of the increasing amount of information becoming available on the Internet are a lack of organization and quality control mechanisms. Hawkins

(1994, p. 25) states: 'The recognition that the amount of information in our society is becoming overwhelming and that we need tools to navigate this information is not new.'

Collection management is still an important and necessary function for the digital library. With traditional print-based collections, there is some degree of control over the collection. In print collections, versions of publications tend to be stable and the collection is usually located in one place, allowing staff to easily determine what is in the collection and where it may be located (Ackerman and Fielding, 1995?). With digital collections, collection management is different since URLs change, content of documents may change, and the location and existence of sites frequently change or disappear. Individuals can exercise direct control only over what is stored in their own local collections. In a digital library, an ongoing effort must be taken to monitor links to other resources and locations. Unfortunately, most libraries are unable to devote the time to such maintenance efforts, despite the fact that unmaintained links prevent access, presenting those libraries which provide unusable links in a poor light. Some of the problems encountered by public users of digital collections and Internet accessible archives are:

- difficulty in finding information due to poor organization and lack of search tools;
- lack of consistency in the presentation of similar information;
- outdated information;
- obvious errors in grammar and spelling;
- too many links to empty or useless information;
- frequent reorganization which forces users to guess where to find previously located references;
- documents not available in formats suitable for both online use and printing.

Pettengill and Arango, 1995)

Converting documents for digital libraries typically begin with a subset of the library's collections. 'Unfortunately, these efforts have often focused on very little used materials, either from a desire to preserve digitally truly rare collections, or from a fear of approaching the digital use of copyrighted materials' (Butler, 1996, p. 126). There are also issues surrounding the longevity of storage mediums used for digital libraries. The technology used to record, store, and retrieve information is constantly changing, and is estimated to have a two to five year life expectancy (Task Force on Archiving of Digital Information, 1995). Technological obsolescence may be a greater concern for digital information than the physical condition of the original material. Maintenance efforts are essential to ensure the stability of the digital collection. 'Backups must be multigenerational, using remote storage, with regular disaster simulations and tests' (Graham, 1995, p. 333).

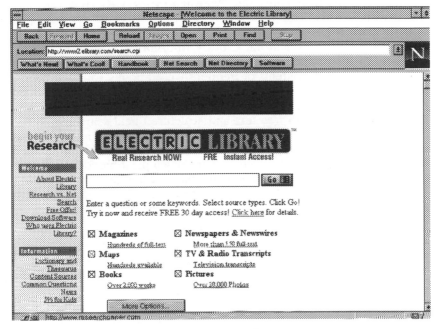

Figure 4.10 Electric Library main page.
Source: *info@infonautics.com.*
Reprinted with permission of Electric Library

Electric Library The Electric Library is a general reference product that provides access to:

- full-text newspapers;
- hundreds of full-text magazines;
- national and international news wires;
- about 2000 complete works of literature;
- over 28000 photographs, images and maps;
- television and radio transcripts;
- book, movie, and software reviews;
- the complete version of *Collier's Encyclopedic CD-ROM*, and reference works such as *Webster's New World Dictionary* and the *World Almanac and Book of Facts.*

Information is updated daily via satellite and other direct links. The Electric Library may be visited on the World Wide Web at http://www2.elibrary.com/search.cgi (See Figure 4.10).

ELINOR The ELINOR project started in 1992 as a joint venture between De Montfort University, Milton Keynes, UK, IBM UK, and the British Library. This was one of the earliest digital projects, it is notable since it has set a standard for subsequent projects. The name ELINOR stands for 'Electronic Library Information Online Retrieval.' The goal of the project was to build an electronic library with a large collection of the full contents of frequently used books, journals, course materials and multimedia learning packages which could be accessed directly via Windows-based PCs and workstations (Zhao, 1994, p. 289). ELINOR supports both free text and structured field searching.

Document capture turned out to be the most labor intensive and consuming part of constructing ELINOR. Project organizers learned that when manual tasks involved in managing a print based library such as check-in and shelving are removed, they are replaced by new tasks like backing up data and printing control (Zhao, 1994, p. 291). Five classes of digital library management were involved in the project:

- management of data – includes filing, indexing, and backing up image and text data;
- management of users – setting up and operating user accounts;
- usage statistics management – collecting, managing, and reporting system resource usage;
- printing management;
- management of the system software and hardware – managing the server, networks, and client software.

(Zhao, 1994, pp. 291–2).

Usage statistics are one of the most important functions for all digital libraries. Interestingly, project organizers were not permitted to scan copyrighted materials into ELINOR unless material usage statistics could be reported to the publishers. Additionally, usage statistics provide important feedback to be used for operating the digital library.

A study to gather user responses to ELINOR was conducted and revealed that users found it quicker to locate information in a digital library, but that it was more difficult to find information in an electronic book as compared to a print version (Zhao, 1994, p. 293). Users also felt that ELINOR was much more useful than OPACs. ELINOR has a World Wide Web server available through the ELINOR Web page, located at http://zaphod.mk.dmu.ac.uk/.

Informedia Informedia is a research initiative at Carnegie Mellon University to study how multimedia digital libraries can be created and used. Informedia was jointly established by Carnegie Mellon University and QED Communications (WQED Pittsburgh). The project integrates regional and national resources and focuses on creating and applying interactive multimedia to learning and communication for K-12 and beyond (Carnegie Mellon University, 1996). Informedia is a large, online digital video library featuring full-content and knowledge-based search and retrieval. Participating libraries will house 1000 hours of edited and unedited documentaries and educational videos from WQED Pittsburgh, Fairfax Count (VA) Public Schools, and the Open University (U.K.). Information on Informedia is available on the World Wide Web at http://www.informedia.cs.cmu.edu/.

Project Open Book This is a project taking place at Yale University to explore the feasibility and costs associated with large scale conversion of preserved materials from microfilm to digital imagery. The project goals are:

* to create a 10 000 volume digital image library;
* to enhance access through document structure and page number indexes; and
* to enhance access to the collection by making it available over the University network and eventually, the Internet.

(Yale University, 1996)

Full-text conversion via optical character recognition (OCR) is not being used at this time. Support for the project has been provided by the Commission on Preservation and Access and the National Endowment for the Humanities. The project has an experimental image server which contains image representations of nineteenth- and twentieth-century books which have been converted for 35 mm preservation microfilm. These books are from Yale's American and European history collections. The image server may be accessed by visiting http://www.library.yale.edu/ preservation/pobex.html. More information on Project Open Book is available on the World Wide Web at http://www.library.yale.edu/preservation.pobweb.htm.

University of Michigan Digital Library This project is a multidisciplinary collaboration between the faculty and library staff at the University of Michigan, and will form a collection based on earth and space sciences. The content of the information will be supplied by participating publishers, including Elsevier Science, UMI International, and McGraw-Hill. The information will be evaluated and tested in high school science classrooms in Ann Arbor, Michigan, at Stuyvesant High School in New York City, in instruction and research at the University of Michigan, and through access provided at Ann Arbor and New York City public libraries. The ultimate goal of the project is to 'help create an environment in which people . . .have on a desktop a personalized ("special") library built upon collections of world wide information sources' (University of Michigan Digital Library, 1996b). Information on the University of Michigan Digital Library is available on the World Wide Web at http://www.sils.umich.edu/UMDL/overview.html.

University of Illinois at Urbana-Champaign Digital Library The goal of this project, which is referred to as 'UIUC DL,' is to develop an 'information infrastructure' to search technical documents on the Internet. The project's test bed consists of engineering and physics journals based in the Grainger Engineering Library. Participating publishers include Academic Press, the American Institute of Physics, the Institute of Electrical and Electronics Engineers, and John Wiley & Sons. Articles are gathered directly from publishers in SGML, and include all text, figures, tables, images, and mathematical equations. The SGML document structure is being used for searching. The articles are being placed in the digital library on a production basis, and the National Center for Supercomputing Applications (NCSA) is 'developing software for the Internet version in an attempt to make server-side repository search widely available' (University of Illinois at Urbana-Champaign, 1996). Information on this project is available on the World Wide Web at http://dli.grainger.uiuc.edu/.

Examination of digital libraries
Lynn-George (1996) describes some of the benefits of digitized information:

• for material that is damaged or deteriorating irreversibly, it offers the opportunity to provide replacement copies that are comparable to those provided through preservation photocopying or microfilming;
• for rare or fragile materials, digitization reduces handling of the original while increasing access through the digital copy;
• image enhancement can correct deficiencies in the original;
• electronic imaging permits high storage density.

Digital libraries protect and preserve materials. Digitization provides users with more possibilities to manipulate information than are offered by traditional print publications. Digital collections serve many users simultaneously, and around the clock in most cases. Lastly, digital resources are always available for use since they cannot be checked out, lost, or stolen.

Conclusion

In his article, 'Planning for the National Electronic Library,' Hawkins (1996) outlines his proposal for a national electronic library which he feels will solve the economic crises facing libraries, use new technology to change scholarship, and bring cultural, social, and economic benefits of information to many. The basic principles for Hawkins' library include: free access; focus on materials and issues which are relevant to the roles of colleges and universities; ability to work with commercial and public organizations which also provide information on the Internet; anticipation of future needs and preservation of the past. Hawkins' model would follow the model of an independent nonprofit organization, yet would not function like a consortium or other cooperative groups. In his plan, Hawkins advocates voluntary participation by libraries to make available electronically those resources for which they own and hold the copyright. The electronic library will in turn make these resources available to users. This library is envisioned as a virtual library with collaboration from institutions throughout the United States. Lastly, Hawkins suggests that OCLC and the Research Libraries Group (RLG) should be subcontracted to offer service to institutions that support local resources. This would use the cataloging expertise of the organizations, reduce duplication, and would help to make cataloging available electronically.

Although Hawkins' vision is feasible, the library and information science profession is not close to implementing such a solution. Such a model is ideal for international cooperation. It could draw on the wealth of resources and expertise provided by individuals around the world and would not have to be limited to the United States to work or be effective. Electronic resources have, however, changed the role of libraries as information providers. Libraries have begun to offer more information, and often on a 24 hour basis, while users increasingly have less direct contact with library professionals. Networked resources and Internet connections have allowed some users to dial into the library from home or other remote locations. Despite the fact that libraries are providing more information than ever, users may rely on the library less as a physical place and more as a resource. Electronic resources have also changed the role of library professionals. Although it was always essential for library professionals to be up-to-date on resources, the pressure is greater than ever. This goal is not easily accomplished due to the rapidly developing and changing nature of electronic resources. Products and services become outdated and obsolete much faster than they did in the past. Electronic resources may force libraries and professionals to keep current, but they also have provided users with a greater variety of current resources that were often only available to those with the equipment necessary to access them.

Chapter 5

Select Bibliography and References

Print Resources

American Association of School Librarians (1996) *How to connect to the Internet.* Chicago: American Library Association

Bristow, A. (1992) Academic reference service over electronic mail. *College & Research Libraries News,* **53**, 631–632, 637

Buckland, M. (1992) *Redesigning library services: a manifesto.* Chicago: American Library Association

Buckland, M. (1995) What will collection developers do? *Information Technology and Libraries,* **14**, 155–159

Butler, B. (1996) Electronic course reserves and digital libraries: progenitor and prognosis. *Journal of Academic Librarianship,* **22**, 124–127

Catenazzi, N. and Sommaruga, L. (1995) An electronic library based on hyper-books: the Hyper-Lib Project. *Online & CDROM Review,* **19(3)**, 127–134

Chachra, V. (1993) Accessing multimedia in virtual libraries. *Information Technology and Libraries,* **12**, 242–245

Crawford, W. and M. Gorman (1995) *Future libraries: dreams, madness & reality.* Chicago: American Library Association

Cunningham, S. and J. Rosebush (1996) *Electronic publishing on CD-ROM.* Bonn: O'Reilly

Demas, S. (1994) Collection development for the electronic library. *Library Hi Tech,* **12(3)**, 71–80

Duranceau, E. *et al.* (1996) Electronic journals in the MIT Libraries: report of the 1995 E-Journal Subgroup. *Serials Review*, **21(4)**, 67–77

Evans, A.K. (1992) Electronic reference services: mediation for the 1990s. *Reference Librarian*, **37**, 75–90

Graham, P. (1995) Requirements for the digital research library. *College & Research Libraries News*, **56**, 331–339

Harden, G. (1994) The virtual library: what is it and where are we headed? *North Carolina Libraries*, 99–101

Harris, H. (1996) Retraining librarians to meet the needs of the virtual library patron. *Information Technology and Libraries*, **15**, 48–52

Hauptman, R. and Anderson, C.L. (1994) The people speak: the dispersion and impact of technology in American libraries. *Information Technology and Libraries*, **13**, 249–256

Hawkins, B. (1994) Creating the library of the future: incrementalism won't get us there! *Serials Librarian*, **24(3/4)**, 17–47

Hunter, K. (1993) The changing business of scholarly publishing. *Journal of Library Administration*, **19(3/4)**, 23–38

Internet directories. In Morville, Rosenfeld, and Janes (1996), pp. 95–117

Jizba, L. *et al.* (1994) (eds) *Guidelines for the bibliographic description of interactive multimedia*. Chicago: American Library Association

Johnson, T. (1994) Spinning the World Wide Web. *Beam Line*, **24(3)**, 2–9

Kahle, B. (1997) Preserving the Internet: an archive of the Internet may prove to be a vital record for historians, businesses, and governments. *Scientific American*, **276**, 82–83

LaGuardia, C. and Bentley, S. (1992) Electronic databases: will old collection development policies still work? *Online*, **16(4)**, 60–63

Lanier, D. and Wilkins, W. (1994) Ready reference via the Internet. *RQ*, **33(3)**, 359–368

Lawley, E.L. and Summerhill, C. (1993) *Internet primer for information professionals: a basic guide to Internet networking technology.* Westport, CT: Meckler

Leon, R.E. (1994) The Internet world: its protocols and mainstream services. *Online and CDROM Review,* **18(4)**, 229–239

Lynch, M.J. (1996) How wired are we? New data on library technology. *College & Research Libraries News,* **57**, 97–100

Magrill, R.M. and Corbin, J. (1989) *Acquisitions management and collection development in libraries* 2nd edn. Chicago: American Library Association

McClements, N. and Becker, C. (1996) Writing Web page standards. *College & Research Libraries News,* **57**, 16–17

Morgan, E. (1995) Description and evaluation of the 'Mr. Serials' process: automatically collecting, organizing, archiving, and disseminating electronic serials. *Serials Review,* **21(4)**, 1–12

Morville, P. (1996a) Internet search tools. In Morville, Rosenfeld, and Janes (1996), pp. 120–216

Morville, P. (1996b) Using the Internet for research. In Morville, Rosenfeld, and Janes (1996), pp. 27–49

Morville, P., Rosenfeld, L., and Janes, J. (1996) (eds) *The Internet searcher's handbook: locating information, people & software.* New York: Neal-Schuman

Neavill, G. and Shéble, M.A. (1995) Archiving electronic journals. *Serials Review,* **21(4)**, 13–21

Parang, E. and Saunders, L. (1994) (compilers) *Spec Kit 201: Electronic journals in ARL libraries: policies and procedures.* Washington, D.C.: Association of Research Libraries

Ramo, J.C. (1996) Winner take all. *Time,* **148(13)**, 57–64

Rowland, F. (1995) The need for information organizations and information professionals in the Internet era. *Serials Review,* **21(1)**, 84–85

Ryan, S. (1996) Using the Internet for reference. In Morville, Rosenfeld, and Janes (1996), pp. 11–26

Saunder, L.M. (1993) (ed.) *The virtual library: visions and realities.* Westport: Meckler

Shaw, D. (1994) Libraries of the future: glimpses of a networked, distributed, collaborative, hyper, virtual world. *Libri,* **44(3)**, 206–223

Shirato, L. (1992) (ed.) *Working with faculty in the new electronic library.* Ann Arbor, Mich.: Learning Resouces and Technologies

Skinner, R. (1995) Multimedia resource access: the 'last frontier.' *Resource Sharing and Information Networks,* 10 **(1–2)**, 101–115

Stoker, D. (1992) Editorial: The electronic library: myth or reality? *Journal of Librarianship and Information Science,* **24**, 183–185

Top Web sites to add interactive multimedia and you can view it through Shockwave. *Information Today,* **13(1)**, 33, 35

Woodward, H. and McKnight, C. (1995) Electronic journals: issues of access and bibliographical control. *Serials Review,* **21(2)**, 71–78

Zhao, D. (1994) The ELINOR Electronic Library System. *Electronic Library,* **12(5)**, 289–294

Online Resources

About jughead (1993) [Online]. Available World Wide Web: gopher:// cheops.anu.edu.au:70/00/Socioinf-query/JugheadVeronica/about-jughead

Academic Press (1996) *IDEAL/APPEAL* [Online]. Available World Wide Web: http://www.apnet.com/www/ap/aboutid.htm

Ackerman, M. and Fielding, R. (1995) *Collection maintenance in digital libraries* [Online]. Available World Wide Web: http://csdl.tamu.edu/ DL95/papers/ackerman/ackerman.html

ADONIS B.V. (1996a) *Home page* [Online]. Available World Wide Web: http://www.adonis.nl/

ADONIS B.V. (1996b) *Electronic journal subscriptions (EJS)* [Online]. Available World Wide Web: http://www.adonis.nl/

ADONIS B.V. (1996c) *Frequently asked questions* [Online]. Available World Wide Web: http://www.adonis.nl/

ADONIS B.V. (1996d) *List of publishers participating in ADONIS* [Online]. Available World Wide Web: http://www.adonis.nl/

ADONIS B.V. (1996e) Advantages of using ADONIS [Online]. Available World Wide Web: http://www.adonis.nl/

Ames Public Library (1996) *Virtual tour* [Online]. Available World Wide Web: http://mirage.scl.ameslab.gov/jc/library/vt.html

Argus Associates (1997) *The Argus Clearinghouse* [Online]. Available World Wide Web: http://www.clearinghouse.net/

Arnold, M. (1997) *Web-based libraries* [Online]. Available World Wide Web: http://www.arts.unimelb.edu.au/fcf/ucr/workshop/qlibrary.htm

Bailey, C.W., Jr. (1997) *Scholarly Electronic Publishing Bibliography* [Online]. Available World Wide Web: http://info.uh.edu/sepb/sepb.html

Barry, T. (1995) *Electronic document delivery – the technical options* [Online]. Available World Wide Web: http://snazzy.anu.edu.au/CNASI/SU/DocDelPres/start.html

Bennett, G. (1995) *The coming of age of VRML* [Online]. Available World Wide Web: http://tcp.ca/Dec95/VRML.html

Berkeley Digital Library SunSITE (1995) *Documents in the digital culture: shaping the future: a report on a workshop held at the Hawaii International Conference on System Sciences, January, 1995* [Online]. Available World Wide Web: http://sunsite.berkeley.edu/Info/Hiconf/

Berners-Lee, T. and Cailliau, R. (1990) *World Wide Web: proposal for a hypertext project* [Online]. Available World Wide Web: http://www.w3.org/pub/WWW/Proposal

Bezy, M. (1996) *Digital libraries for large multimedia collections* [Online]. Available World Wide Web: http://www.software.ibm.com/is/dig-lib/dlip.htm

Blinco, K. (1996) *Some recent initiatives in electronic document delivery* [Online]. Available World Wide Web: http://www.gu.edu.au/alib/iii/docdel/online.htm

Bostock, Stephen (1997) *Searching the Internet: Archie* [Online] Available World Wide Web: http://www.keele.ac.uk/depts/cs/Stephen__ Bostock/Internet/inarchie.htm

Bowker Book Company (1996a) *Bookwire* [Online] Available World Wide Web: http://www.bookwire.com/

Bowker Book Company (1996b) *BookWire Reading Room* [Online]. Available World Wide Web: http://www.bookwire.com/links/ readingroom/readingroom.html

Brent, D. (1995) Stevan Harnad's 'subversive proposal': kick-starting electronic scholarship. *Ejournal* **5(1)**. [Online] Available World Wide Web: http://rachel.albany.edu/~ejournal/v5n1/article.html

British Library Document Supply Centre (1996a) [*Home page*] [Online]. Available World Wide Web: http://portico.bl.uk/dsc/

British Library Document Supply Centre (1996b) Automated requests via *ARTTel* [Online]. Available World Wide Web: http://portico.bl.uk/ dsc/arttel.html

British Library Document Supply Centre (1996c) *Automated requests via ARTE-mail* [Online]. Available World Wide Web: http:// portico.bl.uk/dsc/artemail.html

British Library Document Supply Centre (1996d) *Document delivery services* [Online]. Available World Wide Web: http://portico.bl.uk/dsc/ delivery.html

Carnegie Mellon University (1996) *The Informedia Project* [Online]. Available World Wide Web: http://www.informedia.cs.cmu.edu/

Carl, J. (1995) *Protocol gives sites ways to keep out the 'bots* [Online]. Available World Wide Web: http://www.webweek.com/95Nov/news/ nobots.html

Center for Knowledge Management (1996) *Red Sage Electronic Journal Project: abstract* [Online]. Available World Wide Web: http:// www.ckm.ucsf.edu/Projects/RedSage/

Chapman, S. and Kenney, A.R. (1996) Digital conversion of research library materials: a case for full informational capture. *D-Lib Magazine* [Online]. Available World Wide Web: http://www.dlib.org/dlib/ october96/cornell/10chapman.html

City of Bits WWW Team (1995a) *[City of Bits] Welcome* [Online]. Available World Wide Web: http://www-mitpress.mit.edu/City_of_Bits/welcome.html

City of Bits WWW Team (1995b) *[City of Bits] Welcome from William J. Mitchell* [Online]. Available World Wide Web: http://www-mitpress.mit.edu/City_of_Bits/wjm_welcome.html

Cognitec/3rd Force Software, Inc. (1995) *Alive & free* [Online]. Available World Wide Web: http://www.c3f.com/alivfree.html

Commission on Preservation and Access and the Research Libraries Group (1996) *Preserving digital information: report of the Task Force on Archiving of Digital Information* [Online]. Available World Wide Web: http://www.rlg.org/ArchTF/tfadi.index.htm

Committee on Institutional Cooperation (1996a) *CIC electronic journals collection* [Online]. Available World Wide Web: http://ejournals.cic.net/

Committee on Institutional Cooperation (1996b) *Quick documentation for the Electronic Journals Archive* [Online]. Available World Wide Web: http://ejournals.cic.net/ej.doc.html

Covi, L. and Kling, R. (1996) *Digital shift or digital drift? Dilemmas of managing digital library resources in North American universities* [Online]. Available World Wide Web: http://hsb.baylor.edu/ramsower/acis/papers/covi.htm

Covi, L. (1997) The Future of electronic journals: unpuzzling researcher attitudes about electronic journals. *Revista Española de Bibliologia* [Online]. Available World Wide Web: http://arcano.lib.surrey.ac.uk/%7ejosema/reb/eng/vol1no1/vol1no1b.html

Croft, W.B. (1995) What do people want from information retrieval? *D-Lib Magazine* [Online]. Available World Wide Web: http://www.dlib.org/dlib/november95/11croft.hmtl

Cross, W. (1996) *All-In-One search page* [Online]. Available World Wide Web: http://www.albany.net/allinone

Day, C. (1993) *Economics of electronic publishing (paper presented at the AAUP/ARL symposium on electronic publishing, November, 1993)* [Online]. Available World Wide Web: http://www.press.umich.edu/jep/works/colin.econ.html

Deja News, Inc. (1997) *Deja News* [Online]. Available World Wide Web: http://www.dejanews.com/

Dell, T. (1995) *Online books FAQ of 6/1/93 (added a link on January 26, 1995)* [Online]. Available World Wide Web: http://www.cs. indiana.edu/metastuff/bookfaq.html

Digital Equipment Corporation (1996) *AltaVist search: main page* [Online]. Available World Wide Web: http://altavista.digital.com/

Digital Library (1996) *About the DL* [Online]. Available World Wide Web: http://www.c2.org/~library/about.html

Duncan, D. (1995) Library workers and other professionals: past successes, present problems and future questions. *The Olive Tree* [Online]. Available World Wide Web: http://timon.sir.arizona.edu/ pubs/arts/duncan.html [note: journal is now obsolete]

Earl, L. (1996) *Whither the electronic journal?* [Online]. Available World Wide Web: http://www.lib.ic.ac.uk:8081/leah.htm

Eastgate Systems, Inc. (1996a) *Home page* [Online]. Available World Wide Web: http://www.eastgate.com/

Eastgate Systems, Inc. (1996b) *Readers and writers* [Online]. Available World Wide Web: http://www.eastgate.com/readwrite.html

Eiblum, P. (1995) *The coming of age of document delivery* [Online]. Available World Wide Web: http://www.asis.org/Bulletin/Feb-95/ eiblum.html

ELINOR *Electronic Library* (1996) [Online]. Available World Wide Web: http://zaphod.mk.dmu.ac.uk/

ELINOR Project (1996) *ELINOR Electronic Library Project bibliography* [Online]. Available World Wide Web: http://ford.mk.dmu.ac.uk/ Projects/ELINOR/elinbib.htm

Elsevier Science (1995) *Elsevier Science:' Questions and Answers [About Elsevier Electronic Subscriptions]* [Online]. Available World Wide Web: http://www-east.elsevier.com/ees/qa.htm

Elsevier Science (1996) *TULIP final report* [Online]. Available World Wide Web: http://www.elsevier.nl:80/homepage/about/resproj/trmenu.htm

Emerson, Toni (1997) *VRML Bibliography* [Online]. Available World WideWeb: http://www.hitl.washington.edu/projects/knowledge_base/vrml_bibliography.html

Engineering Information Inc. (1996) *Ei Catalog – Full-text: Ei Document delivery service* [Online]: Available World Wide Web: http://www.ei.org/eihome/catalog/data/fulltext.htm

Excite, Inc. (1996) *Excite navigation service* [Online]. Available World Wide Web: http.//corp.excite.com/excite.html

Excite, Inc. (1997) *WebCrawler Searching* [Online]. Available World Wide Web: http://www.webcrawler.com/

Felt, E. and Scales, J. (1996) *List and analysis of Web robots* [Online]. Available World Wide Web: http://wwwsulibs.wsu.edu/general/robots.htm

Fielding, R. (1994) *Maintaining distributed hypertext info-structures: Welcome to MOMspider's Web* [Online]. Available World Wide Web: http://www.ics.uci.edu/pub/websoft/MOMspider/WWW94/paper.html

Fillmore, L. (1993) *Internet publishing: how we must think* [Online]. Available World Wide Web: http://www.obs-us.com/obs/english/papers/think.htm

Focused Investigation of Document Delivery Options (FIDDO) Project (1996) *Overview of EDD research and services: FIDDO report to eLib* [Online]. Available World Wide Web: http://dils2.lboro.ac.uk/fiddo/report.html

Franks, J. (1993a) *The impact of electronic publishing on scholarly journals* [Online]. Available on World Wide Web: http://cause-www.colorado.edu/information-resources/ir-library/text/cem9410.txt

Franks, J. (1993b) *What is an electronic journal?, Parts 1–4* [Online]. Available World Wide Web: gopher://gopher.cic.net:2000/00/e-serials/About_Electronic_Publishing/what-is-ejournal-1; gopher://gopher.cic.net:2000/00/e-serials/About_Electronic_Publishing/what-is-ejournal-2; gopher://gopher.cic.net:2000/00/e-serials/About_Electronic_Publishing/what-is-ejournal-3; gopher://gopher.cic.net:2000/00/e-serials/About_Electronic_Publishing/what-is-ejournal-4

Franks, M. (1995) *The Internet publishing handbook: for World Wide Web, Gopher, and WAIS.* Reading, Massachusetts: Addison-Wesley

Publishing Company [Online]. Available World Wide Web: http://
www.sscnet.ucla.edu/ssc/franks/book/

Gale Research (1997) *CyberHound* [Online]. Available World Wide
Web: http://www.thomson.com/cyberhound.html

Gladney, H. and Bezy, M. (1996) *Digital intellectual property – protecting
everyone's interests* [Online]. Available World Wide Web: http://www.
software.ibm.com/is/dig-lib/dlrpmb.htm

Global Campus (1996a) *Global Campus* [Online]. Available World
Wide Web: http://www.csulb.edu/gc

Global Campus (1996b) *About the global campus* [Online]. Available
World Wide Web: http://www.csulb.edu/gc/info/index.html

Grewal, Subir (1996) *Extremely Lynx* [Online]. Available World Wide
Web: http://www.crl.com/~subir/lynx.html

Grinstein, G. and Ward, M. (1996) Introduction to visualization: Vis '96
Tutorial#2: Multimedia [Online]. Available World Wide Web: http://
www.cs.uml.edu/~ogrinstei/tut/v96_tut2.html

Grolier Interactive Incorporated (1996a) *Consolidated product list*
[Online]. Available World Wide Web: http://gi.grolier.com/gi/
products/prodlist.html#REFERENCE

Grolier Interactive Incorporated (1996b) *Grolier Online: Grolier Interactive Main Page* [Online]. Available World Wide Web: http://
gi.grolier.com/gi.html

Gromov, G.R. (1996) *The roads and crossroads of Internet's history*
[Online]. Available World Wide Web: http://www.internetvalley.com/
intval.html

Grossan, B. (1996) *Search engines: what they are, how they work, and
practical suggestions for getting the most out of them* [Online]. Available World Wide Web: http://www.webreference.com/content/search/

Guenette, D. and Gustavson, R. (1996) CD-ROM and Web browsers:
HTML as the Lingua Franca? *CD-ROM Professional* [Online]. Available World Wide Web: http://www.onlineinc.com/cdrompro/0896CP/
gustav8.html

Hardenbergh, J. (1996) *VRML frequently asked questions* [Online]. Available World Wide Web: http://vag.vrml.org/VRML_FAQ.html

Harnad, S. (1995a) Electronic scholarly publication: quo vadis? *Serials Review*, **21(1)**. [Online]. Available World Wide Web: ftp://cogsci. ecs.soton.ac.uk/pub/harnad/Harnad/harnad95.quo.vadis

Harnad, S. (1995b) The postGutenberg galaxy: how to get there from here. *Times Higher Education Supplement* [Online]. Available World Wide Web: http://cogsci.ecs.soton.ac.uk:80/~harnad/THES/thes.html

Harris, B. (1996) *Navigating the information superhighway – week 8: Jughead (lecture notes for engineering course)* [Online]. Available World Wide Web: http://pine.shu.ac.uk/~eitrgh/ntiwk8.html

Hart, M. (1995) *History and philosophy of Project Gutenberg* [Online]. Available World Wide Web: http://www.promo.net/pg/history.html

Hawkins, B.L. (1996) Planning for the national electronic library. *Educom Review*, **31(3)** [Online]. Available World Wide Web: http:// www.educom.edu/web/pubs/review/reviewArticles/29319.html

Hitchcock, S., Carr, L. and Hall, W. (1996) *A survey of STM online journals 1990–95: the calm before the storm* [Online]. Available World Wide Web: http://journals.ecs.soton.ac.uk/survey/survey.html

Howe, D. (1996) (ed.) *Free online dictionary of computing* [Online]. Available World Wide Web: http://wombat.doc.ic.ac.uk/

Hughes, K. (1994) *Entering the World Wide Web: a guide to cyberspace* [Online]. Available World Wide Web: http://www.eit.com/web/www. guide/

IBM (1995) *IBM and the Internet: an ancient history* [Online]. Available World Wide Web: http://www.ibm.com/Features/ancient.html

Imperative! (1996) *Domain-name database* [Online]. Available World Wide Web: http://www.internet.org/

Infonautics Corporation (1996a) *Content of the electric library* [Online]. Available World Wide Web: http://www.elibrary.com/info/content. html

Infonautics Corporation (1996b) *Welcome to the Electric Library* [Online]. Available World Wide Web: http://www2.elibrary.com/search. cgi

Infoseek Corporation (1996a) *Company history* [Online]. Available World Wide Web: http://info.infoseek.com/doc/Reference/History. html

Infoseek Corporation (1996b) *Search technology comparison* [Online]. Available World Wide Web: http://info.infoseek.com/doc/Reference/ SearchTech.html

Inglis, A. (1993) *From across the room to across the world: the electronic delivery of formatted documents distinguishing the reality from the myth* [Online]. Available World Wide Web: gopher://gopher.latrobe. edu.au/00/Library%20Services/VALA%20Conference%20Papers/ Inglis.txt

Institute for Scientific Information (1997) *ISI Electronic Library Update* [Online]. Available World Wide Web: http://www.isinet.com/whatsnew/ whatsnew.html

Internet Public Library (1995a) *IPL Internet guide: gopher resource types* [Online]. *Available World Wide Web:* http://www.ipl.org/ classroom/userdocs/gopher/resource.html

Internet Public Library (1995b) *IPL Internet guide: quick gopher reference* [Online]. Available World Wide Web: http://www.ipl.org/ *classroom*/userdocs/gopher/quick.html

Internet Public Library (1995c) *IPL Internet guide: using FTP* [Online]. Available World Wide Web: http://www.ipl.org/classroom/userdocs/ internet/ftp.html

Internet Public Library (1995d) *IPL Internet guide: Web browsers* [Online]. Available World Wide Web: http://www.ipl.org/classroom/ userdocs/internet/browsers.html

Internet Public Library (1995e) *IPL Internet guide: what is gopher?* [Online]. Available World Wide Web: http://www.ipl.org/classroom/ userdocs/gopher/what.html

Internet Public Library (1996a) *Frequently asked questions* [Online]. Available World Wide Web: http://ipl.sils.umich.edu/about/iplfaq.html

Internet Public Library (1996b) *IPL: The Internet Public Library* [Online]. Available World Wide Web: http://www.ipl.org/

Internet Public Library. (1996c) *IPL Web searching* [Online]. Available World Wide Web: http://www.ipl.org/classroom/userdocs/internet/ engines.html

Jog, V. (1995) *Cost and revenue of academic journals: paper-based versus E-journals* [Online]. Available World Wide Web: http://school net2.carleton.ca/biz/economics/vijayjog.html

Johns Hopkins University Press (1996a) *Project Muse: Frequently asked questions* [Online]. Available World Wide Web: http://calliope.jhu. edu/proj_descrip/faq/

Johns Hopkins University Press (1996b) *Project Muse: Press release for subscribing campuses* [Online]. Available World Wide Web: http:// muse.jhu.edu/proj_descrip/campus_pr.html

JSTOR (1996a) *About JSTOR* [Online]. Available World Wide Web: http://www.jstor.org/about/index.html

JSTOR (1996b) *Mission and goals* [Online]. Available World Wide Web: http://www.jstor.org/about/mission.html

JSTOR (1996c) *JSTOR-Phase 1 Pricing and Availability* [Online]. Available World Wide Web: http://www.jstor.org/about/pricing.html

Kabacoff, R. (1996) *Inter-Links* [Online]. Available World Wide Web: http://www.nova.edu/Inter-Links/

Kehoe, B.P. (1992) *Zen and the art of the Internet: a beginner's guide to the Internet* [Online]. Available World Wide Web: http://www.cs. indiana.edu/docproject/zen/zen-1.0_toc.html

Kling, R. and Covi, L. (1995) *Electronic journals and legitimate media in the systems of scholarly communication* The Information society, 11(4), 261–271 [Online]. Available World Wide Web: http:// www.slis.indiana.edu/TIS/Klingej2.html

Knight-Ridder Information, Inc. (1996) *KR SourceOne Main Page* [Online]. Available World Wide Web: http://www.krinfo.com/krsourceone/

Koster, M. (1995) *Robots in the Web: threat or treat?* [Online]. Available

World Wide Web: http://info.webcrawler.com/mak/projects/robots/threat-or-treat.html

Koster, M. (1996) *WWW Robot frequently asked questions* [Online]. Available World Wide Web: http://info.webcrawler.com/mak/projects/robots/faq.html

Kovacs, D.K. and the Directory Team (1995) *Directory of Scholarly and Professional E-Conferences* [Online]. Available World Wide Web: http://n2h2.com/KOVACS/

Kraft, D. (1993) *One journal editor's view of the future of journals: a tour of the present from inside the journal* [Online]. Available World Wide Web: http://www.oclc.org/oclc/research/publications/review94/part4/journal.htm (included as part of OCLC's *Annual review of research*, 1994)

Kriz, H.M. (1995) *Teaching and Publishing in the World Wide Web* [Online]. Available World Wide Web: http://learning.lib.vt.edu/webserv/

Kriz, H.M. (1996) *Windows and TCP/IP for Internet access* [Online]. Available World Wide Web: http://learning.lib.vt.edu/wintcpip/wintcpip.html

Krol, E. and Hoffman, E. (1993) *What is the Internet?* (FYI 20, RFC 1462) [Online]. Available World Wide Web: http://mist.npl.washington.edu/internet.txt

Language Services International (1997) International Internet Statistics [Online]. Available World Wide Web: http://www./silink.com/usage_stats.htm/

Lary, M. (1994) Electronic journals: challenges for the information profession. *LIBRES: Library and Information Science Research Electronic Journal*, **4(4)** [Online] Available World Wide Web: ftp://info.curtin.edu.au/pub/libres/LIBRE4N4/LARY

Lary, M. (1995) Reference services: yesterday and tomorrow. *LIBRES: Library and Information Science Research Electronic Journal*, **5(2)**. [Online] Available World Wide Web: ftp://info.curtin.edu.au/pub/libres/LIBRE5N2/LARY

Libraries of Purdue University (1996) *THOR+: The Virtual Library*

[Online]. Available World Wide Web: http://www.lib.purdue.edu/ vlibrary/index.html

Life on the Internet: Net timeline (1996) [Online]. Available World Wide Web: http://www.pbs.org/internet/history/

Lucier, R.E. and P. Brantley (1995) The Red Sage Project: An Experimental Digital Journal for the Health Sciences: A Descriptive Overview. *D-Lib Magazine* [Online]. Available World Wide Web: http://www.dlib.org/dlib/august95/lucier/08lucier.html

Lycos, Inc. (1996, April 30) *Press releases: Lycos enters the Intranet market* [Online]. Available World Wide Web: http://www.lycos.com/ press/Intranet.html

Lynch, C.A. (1991) *The Z39.50 Protocol in Plain English* [Online]. Available World Wide Web: http://ds.internic.net/z3950/pe-doc.txt

Lynch, C.A. (1997) Searching the Internet. *Scientific American* [Online]. Available World Wide Web: http://www.sciam.com/0397issue/0397 lynch.html

Lynn-George, J. (1996) *Digitization: a literature review and summary of technical processes, applications and issues* [Online]. Available World Wide Web: http://www.library.ualberta.ca/library_html/libraries/law/ digit1.html

Machovec, G. (1997) *Electronic journal market overview – 1997* [Online]. Available World Wide Web: http://www.coalliance.org/reports/ ejournal.htm

Macromedia, Inc. (1996) *Shockwave center* [Online]. Available World Wide Web: http://www.macromedia.com/shockwave/

Marchal, B. (1996) *SGML: executive summary* [Online]. Available World Wide Web: http://www.brainlink.com/~ben/sgml/executive.htm

McBride, K. (1993) *What presidents need to know . . . about the future of university libraries: technology and scholarly communications.* HEI-RAlliance Executive Strategies Report #2. Boulder, CO: CAUSE for the Higher Education Information Resources Alliance. [Online] Available World Wide Web: http://cause-www.niss.ac.uk/collab/ heirapapers/hei0200.html

McBryan, Oliver (1997) *WWWW- World Wide Web Worm* [Online]. Available World Wide Web: http://wwww.cs.colorado.edu/wwww

McCarty, W. (1997) *Overview of electronic publication* [Online]. Available World Wide Web: http://www.kcl.ac.uk/kis/schools/hums/ruhc/ohc/overview.html

McKinley Group, Inc. (1997) *Welcome to Magellan!* [Online]. Available World Wide Web: http://www.mckinley.com

Meroz, Y. (1995) *VRML: Virtual Reality Modeling Language* [Online]. Available World Wide Web: http://ils.unc.edu/yael/VRML.html

Microsoft Corporation. (1996) *Microsoft Internet Explorer* [Online]. Available World Wide Web: http://www.microsoft.com/ie/

MIT Press (1996) *Electronic books* [Online]. Available World Wide Web: http://mitpress.mit.edu/e–books/

Mitchell, W.J. (1995) *City of bits: space, place and the infobahn.* Cambridge: MIT Press [Online]. Available World Wide Web: http://mitpress.mit.edu/e–books/City_of_Bits/

Mitchell, W.J. (1996) *Homer to home-page: designing digital books* [Online]. Available World Wide Web: http://mitpress.mit.edu/e–books/City_of_Bits_Text_Unbound/text_unbound.html

Naples Area Bulletin Board Operators (1996) *Local bulletin board systems* (1996) [Online]. Available World Wide Web: http://www.naples.net/remote/zrbbs.htm

National Center for Supercomputing Applications (1996) *A beginner's guide to HTML* [Online]. Available World Wide Web: http://www.ncsa.uiuc.edu/General/Internet/WWW/HTMLPrimer.html

Netscape Communications Corporation (1997) *Netscape Navigator Family* [Online]. Available World Wide Web: http://home.netscape.com/comprod/products/navigator/index.html

NEXOR Ltd. (1997) *List of WWW Archie Services* [Online]. Available World Wide Web: http://pubweb.nexor.co.uk/archie/

NEXOR Ltd. (1995) *Welcome to ALIWEB* [Online]. Available World Wide Web: http://www.nexor.co.uk/public/aliweb/aliweb.html

OCLC Online Computer Library Center, Inc. (1996a) *OCLC Electronic Journals Online (EJO): About EJO* [Online]. Available World Wide Web: http://medusa.prod.oclc.org:3050/html/ejo_homepage.htm

OCLC Online Computer Library Center, Inc. (1996b) *OCLC Electronic Journals Online: introducing OCLC Electronic Journals Online: to the next stage of the electronic library* [Online]. Available World Wide Web: http://www.oclc.org/oclc/promo/9449ejob/9449ejob.htm [No longer available]

OCLC Online Computer Library Center, Inc. (1996c) *OCLC Electronic Journals Online: [journals list]* [Online]. Available World Wide Web: http://www.oclc.org/oclc/promo/ejo_list.htm [No longer available]

Odlyzko, A. (1996) *On the road to electronic publishing* [Online]. Available World Wide Web: http://www.research.att.com/~amo/doc/tragic. loss.update

Online Designs, Inc. (1996) *Welcome to i-Explorer* [Online]. Available World Wide Web: http://www.i-explorer.com/home.dll

Open Text Corporation (1996) *The Open Text Index- frequently asked questions* [Online]. Available World Wide Web: http://index.opentext. net/main/faq.html

Open Text Corporation (1997) *The Open Text Index* [Online]. Available World Wide Web: http://index.opentext.net/

OverDrive Systems, Inc. (1996) *Welcome to the Electronic Book Aisle* [Online]. Available World Wide Web: http://www.bookaisle.com/cgi-eba/addlogo.exe?template=main.htm+retailer=overdrv

Ovid Technologies (1996) *ABI/INFORM Global Edition* [Online]. Available World Wide Web: http://www.ovid.com/db/databses/ infodb.htm

Oxford University Press (1996) *OUP Home Page* [Online]. Available World Wide Web: http://www.oup.co.uk/njls/

Pepper, S. (1996) *The Whirlwind guide to SGML tools and vendors* [Online]. Available World Wide Web: http://www.falch.no/people/ pepper/SGML-Tools/

Perrin, W. (1997) *Summary of results: survey of attitudes to electronic books* [Online]. Available at 100617.772@compuserve.com

Pescovitz, D. (1995) The future of libraries. *Wired* [Online]. Available World Wide Web: http://www.hotwired.net/wired/3.12/departments/reality.check.html

Peters, P.E. (1995) Digital libraries are much more than digitized collections. *Educom Review*, **30(4)** [Online]. Available World Wide Web: http://ww.educom.edu/web/pubs/review/reviewArticles/30411.html

Pettengill, R. and Arango, G. (1995) *Four lessons learned from managing World Wide Web digital libraries* [Online]. Available World Wide Web: http://csdl.tamu.edu/DL95/papers/pettengill/pettengill.html

PICK: Quality Internet Resources in Library and Information Science selected by the Thomas Parry Library (1996) *Styles of electronic journals* [Online]. Available World Wide Web: http://www.aber.ac.uk/~tplwww/ej/styles.html

Princeton University Press (1997) *Books online* [Online]. Available World Wide Web: http://pup.princeton.edu/books/

Pullinger, D. and Baldwin, C. (1996) SuperJournal: a project in the UK to developmultimediajournals.*D-LibMagazine*[Online].AvailableWorld Wide Web: http://www.dlib.org/dlib/january96/briefings/01super.html

The Red Sage Project (1996) [Online]. Available World Wide Web: http://www.library.ucsf.edu/lib/gen/redsage.html [Obsolete URL. Red Sage has been superceded by Galen II, available at http://www.library.uscf.edu/hlp/aboutgalen.html

Research Libraries Group (1996a) *ABI/INFORM, Global Edition (ABI)* [Online]. Available World Wide Web: http://www.rlg.org/cit-abi.html

Research Libraries Group (1996b) *Ariel* [Online]. Available World Wide Web: http://www.rlg.org/ariel.html

Research Libraries Group (1996c) *CitaDel* [Online]. Available World Wide Web: http://www.rlg.org/citadel.html

Research Libraries Group (1996d) *Ei Page One (EIP)* [Online]. Available World Wide Web: http://www.rlg.org/cit-eip.html

Research Libraries Group (1996e) *Eureka* [Online]. Available World Wide Web: http://www.rlg.org/eureka.html

Research Libraries Group (1996f) *Inside Information PLUS (IIN)* [Online]. Available World Wide Web: http://www.rlg.org/cit-iin.html

Research Libraries Group (1996g) *Newspaper Abstracts (NPA)* [Online]. Available World Wide Web: http://www.rlg.org/cit-npa.html

Research Libraries Group (1996h) *Periodical Abstracts, Research II Edition (PRA)* [Online]. Available World Wide Web: http://www.rlg.org/cit-pra.html

Rohwedder, W.J. and Alm, A. (1994) *EE Toolbox – workshop resource manual: using computers in environmental education: interactive multimedia and online learning: section II, interactive multimedia* [Online]. Available World Wide Web: http://nceet.snre.umich.edu/Computers/im.html#InteractiveMultimedia

Rowland, F. (1994) Electronic journals: neither free nor easy. *Ejournal*, **4(2)**. [Online] Available World Wide Web: http://poe.acc.virginia.edu/~pm9k/libsci/rowland.html

San Diego Supercomputer Center (1997) *The VRML Repository* [Online] Available World Wide Web: http://www.sdsc.edu/vrml/

Schutzer, D. (1996) A need for a common infrastructure: digital libraries and electronic commerce. *D-Lib Magazine* [Online] Available World Wide Web: http://www.dlib.org/dlib/april96/04schutzer.html

Scott, Peter (1992) Using HYTELNET to access Internet resources. *Public-Access Computer Systems Review*, **3(4)**, 15–21. [Online] Available World Wide Web: http://info.lib.uh.edu/pr/v3/n4/scott.3n4

Scott, Peter (1996) *Free-Nets & Community Networks* [Online] Available World Wide Web: http://www.usask.ca/alternate__views.html

SGML Project (1996) *What is SGML and why should I use it?* [Online]. Available World Wide Web: http://sil.org/sgml/exetwhat.html

Sherwood, K.D. (1996) *A beginner's guide to effective e-mail* [Online]. Available World Wide Web: http://www.webfoot.com/advice/email.top.html

da Silva, Stephanie (1997) *Publicly Accessible Mailing Lists* [Online]. Available World Wide Web: http://www.neosoft.com/internet/paml/index.html

Squier, J. (1996) *The Place* [Online]. Available World Wide Web: http://gertrude.art.uiuc.edu/ludgate/the/place/place2.html

SuperJournal Project (1997) *Home Page* [Online]. Available World Wide Web: http://www.superjournal.ac.uk/sj/project.htm

Tagler, J. (1995) *Delivery of electronic journals: a varied menu* [Online]. Available World Wide Web: http://online.anu.edu.au/CNASI/pubs/OnDisc95/docs/ONL19.html

Task Force on Archiving of Digital Information (1995) *Preserving digital information* [Online]. Available World Wide Web: http://www.rlg.org/ArchTF/tfadi.index.htm#contents

Trade Wave Corporation (1997) *Galaxy* [Online]. Available World Wide Web: http://galaxy.tradewave.com/galaxy.html

Treloar, A. (1995) *Electronic scholarly publishing and the World Wide Web* [Online]. Available World Wide Web: http://elmo.scu.edu.au/sponsored/ausweb/ausweb95/papers/publishing/treloar/

UCLA-NSF Social Aspects of Digital Libraries Workshop: final report (1996) [Online]. Available World Wide Web: http://www.gslis.ucla.edu/DL/UCLA_DL_Report.html

UMI (1996a) *ProQuest Direct on the Web* [Online]. Available World Wide Web: http://pqdbeta.umi.com/ad/pdirect/

UMI (1996b) *UMI InfoStore* [Online]. Available World Wide Web: http://www.umi.com/infostore

UnCover Company (1996) *What is UnCover?* [Online]. Available World Wide Web: http://www.carl.org/uncover/what.html

University of California, San Francisco and Center for Knowledge Management (1997) *Red Sage Experiment concluded* [Online]. Available World Wide Web: http://redsage.ucsf.edu/ [Obsolete. Superceded by Galen II]

University of Illinois at Urbana-Champaign (1996) *UIUC Digital Library Initiative* [Online]. Available World Wide Web: http://dli.grainger.uiuc.edu/

University of Michigan Digital Library (1996a) *University of Michigan*

Digital Library Project Overview [Online]. Available World Wide Web: http://www.sils.umich.edu/UMDL/overview.html

University of Michigan Digital Library (1996b) *University of Michigan Digital Library Project Proposal* [Online]. Available World Wide Web: http://www.sils.umich.edu/UMDL/proposal/summary.html

Vander Meer, P.F., Poole, H. and Van Valey, T. (1997) Are library users also computer users?: a survey of faculty and implications for services. *Public-Access Computer Systems Review,* **8(1)** [Online]. Available World Wide Web: http://info.lib.uh.edu/pr/v8/n1/vanderme. 8n1

Varian, H.R. (1996) Pricing electronic journals. *D-Lib Magazine* [Online]. Available World Wide Web: http://www.dlib.org/dlib/june96/ 06varian.html

VIVA (1996) *VIVA: The Virtual Library of Virginia home page* [Online]. Available World Wide Web: http://www.viva.lib.va.us/

Wactler, H.D., Kanade, T., Smith, M.A., Stevens, S.M. (1996) *Intelligent access to digital video: Informedia Project* [Online]. Available World Wide Web: http://www.computer.org/pubs/computer/dli/r50046/r50046. htm

Wascana Institute (1996) *Library Tutor: an interactive multimedia resource* [Online]. Available World Wide Web: http://www.pcs.sk.ca/ libtutor/

Waters, J. (1996) *Electronic technologies and preservation* [Online]. Available World Wide Web: http://www-cpa.stanford.edu/cpa/reports/ waters2.html

Wimsey Information Services. (1994) *Usenet* [Online]. Available World Wide Web: http://vanbc.wimsey.com/~helpdesk/Info/usenet.html

World Wide Web Consortium (1995a) *A Little History of the World Wide Web* [Online]. Available World Wide Web: http://www.w3.org/ pub/WWW/History.html

World Wide Web Consortium (1995b) *World Wide Web Related Newsgroups* [Online]. Available World Wide Web: http://www.w3.org/pub/ WWW/Newsgroups.html

World Wide Web Consortium (1997) *Web Style Sheets* [Online]. Available World Wide Web: http://www.w3.org/pub/WWW/Style/

Yahoo! Inc. (1995) *Yahoo! history* [Online]. Available World Wide Web: http://www.yahoo.com/docs/pr/history.html

Yahoo! Inc. (1996a) *Yahoo!: Arts: Humanities: Literature: Genres: Web published fiction: Works* [Online]. Available World Wide Web: http://www.yahoo.com/Arts/Humanities/Literature/Genres/Web__Published__Fiction/Works/

Yahoo! Inc. (1996b) *Yahoo!: Recreation: Games: Interactive Fiction* [Online]. Available World Wide Web: http://www.yahoo.com/Recreation/Games/Interactive__Fiction/

Yahoo! Inc. (1997) *Yahoo!* [Online]. Available World Wide Web: http://www.yahoo.com/

Yale University (1996) *Project Open Book* [Online]. Available World Wide Web: http://www.library.yale.edu/preservation/pobweb.htm

Yale University Library (1997) *Background on Project Open Book* [Online]. Available World Wide Web: http://www.library.yale.edu/preservation/pobbkgd.htm

Glossary

ADONIS: A company which offers two services: Electronic Journal Subscriptions (EJS) and Docment Delivery (DD). EJS is a CD-ROM electronic subscription service, and DD is a CD-ROM document delivery service.

aggregator: An intermediate service which offers subscribers electronic titles from different publishers through one interface.

Alive and Free: A page of links to recent free online literature from living authors.

ALIWEB: Search engine created to fill the services provided by Web harvesters and wanders without placing a strain on network and processing standards. Created in 1993 by NEXOR Ltd.

All-In-One Search Page: Grouping of a variety of forms-based Internet search tools created by William Cross.

Alta Vista: Search engine created by Digital Equipment Corporation. Accessible via any standard Web browser.

anonymous FTP: An interactive service available through Internet hosts; allows users to transfer documents, files, programs, and other archived data using FTP. Users log into sites as 'ftp' or 'anonymous.'

APPEAL: A site license for large consortia, available from Academic Press. Provides access at all sites within a consortium to all journal titles formerly held in print locations anywhere within the consortium.

archie: An indexed dictionary of all anonymous FTP archives on the Internet; initially implemented by the McGill University School of Computer Science.

Argus Clearinghouse: Formerly known as the *Clearinghouse for Subject-Oriented Internet Resource Guides.* Holds or points to over 400 guides to Internet-based information resources.

American Standard Code for information Interchange (ASCII): The most commonly used character set for encoding text which uses seven bits for each character, allowing for the inclusion of lower case letters but does not provide letters or other letter forms not used in English.

book-like interface: Method of presenting information in electronic library collections which presents information in a book format; popular with users since information is structured in a format which is familiar to them.

bookmark: Facility which permits users to add an eletronic address (URL) and associated name to a local file to which a user can subsequently refer. The file contains direct links to selected electronic addresses of previously viewed documents.

BookWire: Publisher which provides information on electronic books (fiction, nonfiction/reference, and children's books) as well as background information on authors and an index to author websites.

browser: Program which allows users to read hypertext and to navigate between sites on the World Wide Web. Available on individual workstations, and allow users to send requests to servers or to follow links provided in a document or site. Primarily graphical but some character-based browsers are also available. Lynx, Mosaic, Netscape Navigator, and Microsoft Internet Explorer are examples. Also known as web browsers.

bulletin board: System consisting of a computer and related software which provide an electronic database where users may log-in and post messages or read messages left by other participants.

CitaDel: A citation and document delivery system provided by the Research Libraries Group (RLG) which provides information taken from general and special interest databases.

City of Bits: An electronic book, available via the World Wide Web, which was designed as a companion to the print book of the same title by William J. Mitchell, Dean of the School of Architecture and Planning, MIT.

client: Computer which requests a service from another computer (the server).

client-server system: System which uses software to provide client and server functions.

Committee on Institutional Cooperation (CIC): Academic consortium of members of the Big Ten athletic conference and the University of Chicago.

Committee on Institutional Cooperation's Electronic Journals Collection (CIC-EJC): Collection of electronic journals provided to member libraries of the CIC.

Cyberhound: Search engine created by Gale Research which relies on manual indexing of Internet sites by editors.

Deja News: A World Wide Web interface to Usenet newsgroups; allows users to search Usenet postings, and to read and post to Usenet newsgroups.

digital library: A collection which combines bibliographic description and full-text or image representations of published works.

Digital Library: An online electronic library that provides access to nonfiction, poetry, and short fiction. Also known as 'DL.'

direct access: Navigation method used for digital documents which provides access to specific locations, such as the table of contents, lists of figures or tables.

discussion list: see listserv.

distributed system: A system in which the distribution of functions, available from a number of machines, is transparent to users; the system appears to function like one local machine.

domain: The suffix of a host computer's unique name that is assigned at the highest level; may be shared by other computers within an organization. For example: rutgers.edu is the domain name used for computers within an organization, such as mbfecko@rci.rutgers.edu.

Eastgate Systems: A publisher which solicits hypertext fiction and non-fiction. Also provides Storyspace, a hypertext writing environment which allows authors to create texts that may be freely distributed without royalty.

Electric Library: A general reference product available on the World Wide Web which provides access to full-text newspapers and magazines, news wires, television and radio transcripts, and electronic reference works.

Electronic Book Aisle: A searchable interactive catalog of electronic books; users can view book covers, jackets, author profiles, and tables of contents.

Electronic Document Delivery Integrated Solution (EDDIS): A UK-based project which aims to produce an integrated document delivery system driven by end users, and will include holdings and an article delivery system.

electronic journal: A journal made available electronically via the Internet, World Wide Web, or on CD-ROM. May also be available in print, may supercede a print version, or may be available exclusively in an electronic form.

Electronic Library Information Online Retrieval (ELINOR): A joint venture between De Montfort University, Milton Keynes, UK, IBM UK, and The British Library; one of the earliest digital projects. The project goal was to build an electronic library with a collection of full contents of books, journals, course materials and multimedia learning packages which could be accessed directly via Windows-based PCs and workstations.

electronic mail (e-mail): System which allows for the sharing of online electronic messages among individuals or groups of individuals via a computer network.

Elsevier Electronic Subscriptions (EES): A pilot project which provides electronic versions of Elsevier's print titles and offers libraries complete electronic editions in addition to, or in place of, print titles.

emoticon: A symbol used in an electronic mail message to indicate a facial expression, emotional state, or physical attribute (glasses, braces on teeth, for example). Also known as a 'smilie' :-) :-0 :)

Excite: An Internet navigation service which searches and summarizes more than 50 million Web pages and more than two weeks of Usenet news.

FIDDO: A UK-based project to provide library and information managers with information to permit them to make decisions regarding the feasibility, selection, and implementation of electronic document delivery systems for their institutions.

File Transfer Protocol (FTP): A client-server protocol which allows users to transfer files from one computer to another.

freenet: A community-based information system offering services ranging from e-mail to information services, interactive communications, and conferencing.

Galaxy: A directory and search engine created by the TradeWave Corporation that works with Netscape Navigator and Mosaic browsers and servers.

Global Campus Project: A collaboration between the California State University campuses at Long Beach, San José, Chico, and Cal Poly San Luis Obispo and other institutions to build an electronic global campus which will be available to anyone using the Internet. Contains a variety of educational materials (images, sound, text, and video) to be used for nonprofit educational purposes.

gopher: A distributed document retrieval system consisting of a menu-driven software that searches the Internet for information. Information in gopher systems is organized in a hierarchy of subject-oriented menus which provide links to text files, other menus, binary files, FTP and Telnet sites, and Z39.50 sites.

graphical user interface (GUI): An operating system which relies on icons, or pictures, to represent functions of a particular system; a program with a GUI requires Windows.

harvester: See robot.

hierarchical navigation: Navigation used in electronic library collections which provides links from the table of contents in a digital document.

host: A computer connected to a network, or the computer to which one is connected when using a terminal emulator program.

hostname: Name by which a computer is known on a network.

Hytelnet: A hypertext browser that allows users to access all telnet-accessible sites on the Internet. Developed by Peter Scott of the University of Saskatchewan Libraries.

hypertext: Text that contains links which allow readers to move easily from one document to another with the aid of an interactive browser program.

hypertext-based interface: Method of presenting documents in electronic library collections which relies on hypertext links.

Hypertext Markup Language (HTML): A document format, invented by Tim Berners-Lee of the European Particle Physics Laboratory, or CERN. Uses tags to indicate the different parts or elements of a document.

IDEAL: An electronic service which includes the complete 1996 runs of 175 journals published by Academic Press. Some 1995 issues are included; about 2000 articles are added monthly.

i-Explorer: A search engine that provides access to sites which have been submitted to its database.

image-based interface: Process for presenting information in electronic library collections; typically used when documents are converted from an existing print collection. The benefit of this approach is that it preserves the integrity of the original document.

InfoBike: A UK-based project designed to provide end users with the ability to conduct database searches, electronically request items, and to have full-text items delivered directly to their desktops.

Informedia: A research initiative undertaken by Carnegie Mellon University, Pittsburgh, to study how multimedia digital libraries can be created and used; the project goal is to contain over a thousand hours of digital video, audio, images, text, and related materials.

Infoseek: Search engine which offers both search and directory services.

InfoStore: A full-service document supplier provided by UMI which can provide journal articles, dissertations, technical reports, and conference proceedings.

InfoTrac: A subject and author index to general interest magazines and scholarly journals. It was originally made available on CD-ROM circa 1985.

interactive multimedia: Media which reside in one or more physical carriers, such as videodiscs, computer disks, computer optical discs, etc., or on computer networks. Interactive multimedia are user-controlled, employ nonlinear navigation using computer technology, and the media are manipulated by the user to control the order or nature of the presentation. No two users will have the same experience using interactive multimedia.

interface: A means by which two systems communicate. It can be a piece of hardware or a protocol used to facilitate communication between two software systems.

Internet: A worldwide computer network which connects many smaller networks worldwide.

Internet Public Library: A virtual library with the mission of finding, evaluating, selecting, organizing, and creating quality information sources.

InterNIC (Internet Network Information Center): A collaboration between AT&T, General Atomics, and Network Solutions which began in 1993. The InterNIC Registration Service provides registration services for domain administrators, network coordinators, Internet service providers, and others actively involved with the Internet.

JSTOR: Product originally produced by William G. Bowen, President of the Mellon Foundation, as a solution for libraries which lacked adequate space to store back issues of scholarly journals.

Jughead (Jonzy's Universal Gopher Hierarchy Excavation and Display): A database of gopher links; searches and indexes all gopher sites includes only high-level menu items. Developed in 1993 by University of Utah Computer Center.

KR SourceOne: A service provided by Knight-Ridder Information, Inc., that delivers information from a worldwide collection of libraries with more than 1.5 million titles.

library information system (LIS): A computerized system that provides access to a library's holdings, access to networked databases, and provides access to the Internet, e-mail, and the World Wide Web. Has succeeded the online public access catalog, or OPAC.

Library Tutor: An interactive program designed by Wascana Institute of Regina, Saskatchewan, Canada, to teach students how to use a library.

linear navigation: Navigation method for digital documents which provides forward and backwards movement through documents.

listserv: An automated mailing list dedicated to a particular issue or discipline.

local area network (LAN): A network of computer terminals or microprocessors typically limited to one building or a narrowly defined geographic area.

Lycos: Search engine created by Carnegie Mellon University and later spun off for further development through Lycos, Inc. One of the more popular and well known search engines.

Lynx: Browser commonly used for text-based access to the World Wide Web. Developed at the University of Kansas.

Magellan: Online Internet guide and search engine developed by McKinley Group, Inc.

Microsoft Internet Explorer: Graphical Web browser produced by Microsoft Corporation; released circa 1995.

mirror site: An archival Internet site which is used to store copies of some or all of the files from the original site, making them available more quickly to local users. It also reduces the load on a particular site by making a number of sites available. Mirror sites are typically located in a number of countries worldwide.

mixed strategy: Interface which employs a combination of two or more of the following interfaces: plain text, image-based, hypertext-based, or book-like.

Mosaic: The first multimedia graphical user interface to the Web (circa 1993); developed by Marc Andreesen and Eric Bina at the National Center for Supercomputing Applications.

Multi-User Domain (MUD): A multi-user game which is played over a computer network.

Multi-User Object Oriented Domain (MOO): A text-based multi-user virtual reality game.

Netscape Navigator: Graphical Web browser; produced by Netscape Communications Corporation.

netnews: See Usenet.

network: A communication system that relies on hardware and software.

OCLC Electronic Journals Online (OCLC-EJO): An online service that provides access to 48 journals available via the Internet or through dial access. Access is provided through Guidon, PC-based software developed by OCLC for use with Microsoft Windows.

Online Public Access Catalog (OPAC): A computerized catalog of a library's holdings. It is typically an automated version of the card catalog. Now more frequently known as Library Information System, or LIS.

Open Text Index: Search engine which offers simple and advanced searching capabilities; also available in several languages, including Japanese, Portuguese, and Spanish.

plain text interface: The simplest and most immediate method of presenting information for an electronic library collection. Uses ASCII text, and no images or multimedia images are included. Permits universal accessibility of documents.

Project Gutenberg: An electronic book project founded by Michael Hart which was created with the goal of making texts available in the simplest and easiest to use forms at affordable prices. Texts are made available in ASCII.

Project Muse: An experiment which makes available to libraries scholarly electronic journals published by Johns Hopkins University Press.

Project Open Book: Project undertaken at Yale University, New Haven, Connecticut, to explore the feasibility and costs associated with large-scale conversion of preserved materials from microfilm to digital imagery.

ProQuest: A service from UMI that offers full-text or full-image documents, or can combine searchable text with graphs, charts, maps, and photographs.

Red Sage Project: Collaboration between the University of California,

San Francisco, AT&T Bell Laboratories, and Springer-Verlag which began in 1993 and concluded in 1997 to provide faculty, students, and staff with online access to an electronic library of biomedical and clinical journals.

robot: Program used to roam the World Wide Web and to index sites. Also known as a 'harvester,' 'spider,' and 'web crawler.'

search engine: A program which permits users to do keyword searaching on the Internet.

server: Computer which provides a service or information to another computer which has made a request (the client).

spider: See robot.

Standard Generalized Markup Language (SGML): A standard for electronic information exchange; first produced in 1988, and was used initially for special or complex document management. Uses markup to indicate nature, function, or content of data in a document. The most common application of SGML is HTML.

SuperJournal: A collaborative project between United Kingdom publishers, universities, and libraries to develop multimedia electronic journals.

telnet: An Internet program which allows users to log onto a remote computer; the remote computer is referred to as the 'host.' Telnet allows an individual's computer to become a terminal connected to a remote computer through a process called 'terminal emulation.'

terminal emulator: A program which allows a computer to function like, or emulate, a specific terminal type that is recognized by the host computer.

THOR+: The virtual library of the Libraries of Purdue University which provides access to a virtual reference desk as well as subject reading rooms, electronic journals, and libraries worldwide.

Transmission Control Protocol/Internet Protocol (TCP/IP): Two protocols which are used together as a set of rules for sending information over the Internet.

transverse navigation: Navigation method used for digital documents which provides links across the document as well as across the digital collection.

UnCover: An online periodical article delivery service which indexes almost 17 000 English language periodicals.

Uniform Resource Locator (URL): Protocol used to specify the location of an object or site on the Internet. Commonly referred to as a 'Web address.' For example: http://wfn-shop.Princeton.EDU/foldoc/

(The) University Licensing Project (TULIP): A collaboration between Elsevier Science and a number of American universities. The project's goal was to jointly test systems for networked delivery to, and use of journals at, the user's desktop. The project ran from 1991–1996.

University of Illinois at Urbana-Champaign Digital Library (UIUC DL): Project to develop an information infrastructure to search technical documents on the Internet.

University of Michigan Digital Library: A multidisciplinary collaboration between the faculty and library staff at the University of Michigan to form a collection based on earth and space sciences.

Usenet: Also known as Netnews; a collection of several hundred bulletin boards which use a common distribution method and similar software for posting and reading messages. Individual bulletin boards are generally known as newsgroups, or groups.

Veronica (Very Easy Rodent-Oriented Net-wide Index to Computerized Archives): An indexing tool for gopher menus; often found on the 'other gophers' menu. Maintains an index of gopher menu titles and uses keywords to search those titles.

virtual library: A set of links to various resources on the Internet, such as documents, software, or databases. The links are transparent to users, and they are provided with one interface to information.

Virtual Reality Modeling Language (VRML): Standard used to author, view, and hyperlink three-dimensional images on the World Wide Web. Not an extension, and not virtual reality.

VIVA: A consortium of the libraries of the 39 state supported colleges and universities in Virginia; its mission is to provide access to library and information resources for the Commonwealth of Virginia's academic libraries. Includes electronic books and texts, image databases, electronic journals, and electronic reference works.

web crawler: See robot.

Web Crawler: Search engine and directory operated by America Online. Builds a selective but comprehensive index of the World Wide Web.

Wide Area Information Server (WAIS): A distributed information retrieval system which can retrieve information from the Internet using natural language searching; allows users to search a number of sites simultaneously. Originally released in 1991; designed specifically for maintaining and searching databases.

Windows: A type of software which divides a computer's screen into several boxes which allow users to run different application programs. Windows programs are typically accessed by using a mouse or comparable pointing device.

World Wide Web (WWW): A client-server application which is part of the Internet. Relies on hypertext to provide access to documents and to navigate between documents. It also includes audio and video capabilities as well as the ability to transmit images.

World Wide Web Worm (WWWW): Internet search engine that builds its index from URLs that are referenced by some other URL already known to WWWW.

Yahoo!: Database of links to the World Wide Web and Internet resources, organized as a hierarchical subject-oriented guide. The search engine Alta Vista is used to search Yahoo!

Z39.50: An information retrieval protocol developed by the National Information Standards Organization which is used for communication between databases. Provides a single user interface for the multiple information resources available on the Web. Also known as ISO Z39.50.

Index